About

*I*t's a pretentious thing to do, I know – it would irritate me. What right has this Richard Miles Brown person to pontificate about the mighty universe?

And, talking of pretentiousness, what's with the Miles thing?

My mother's maiden name; all eight of us had it bestowed, including the girls. Our female progenitor thought, rightly of course, that there's an army of Browns in the world and that we might be glad of a device for narrowing identification. A cheap attempt at double-barrelment? I don't think Cecelia Frances Miles was a snob and in her belated honour I make use of the device here, with a friendly wave to the zillions of those other Richard Browns who no doubt will mostly understand.

Our parents caused us to be Catholics, devoutly so in my case to the point where I pondered long and hard about joining the priesthood.

Two years at Ruskin College, Oxford from the age of 24 put paid to that, with rationality being reinforced by an ensuing degree in philosophy and psychology courtesy of New College. I was offered a two year option, instead of the customary three, which I took and, though 'twas taxing, I did well enough to be offered the chance of post-graduate study.

I turned this down because I was disaffected with the extant style of Oxford philosophy. Since renouncing Catholicism I had been looking for an alternative system of belief and, finding nothing which satisfied, had started to devise a bespoke theory. I suppose it's unsurprising that my desire to do metaphysics was not welcomed by the university authorities; one analytical academic had spent years working on a definition of the word 'knowledge' and I would have been expected to do something similar. Thanks but no.

So, I became a late-shift telephone operator and did my own metaphysical thing. The outcome, three years later, was a self-published slim pamphlet simply entitled 'A Theory of the Universe' which, like Hume's treatise, 'fell stillborn from the press.'

Needing to live a little more I took on a 'proper job' but never quite stopped working on the theory.

And then came the internet... With the entirely necessary input of an early webmaster the theory was launched into the ether: **www.universetheory.com** and it has been there ever since.

So, the ideas have been tested and refined to the point where this handy book could be confidently produced in the hope that some might find it useful...

...at least that's my story.

Richard Miles Brown

Something to Believe

Richard Miles Brown

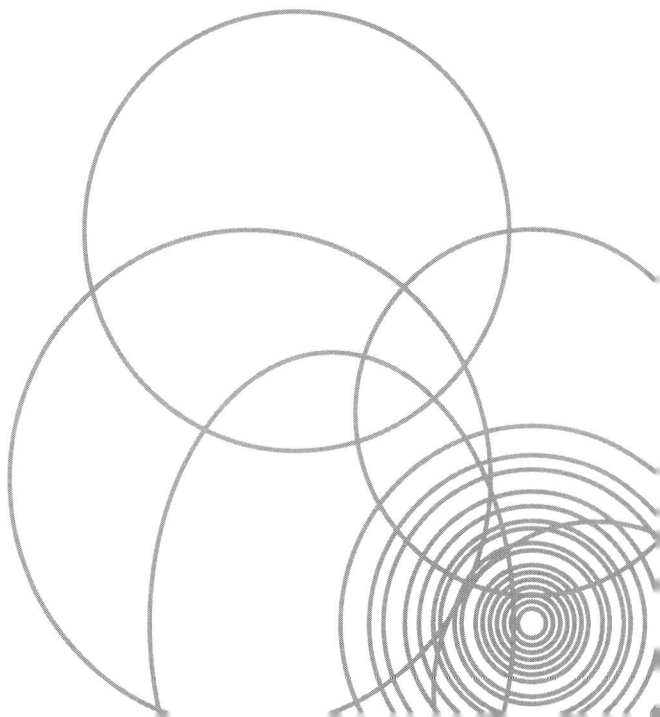

First published in 2013 by
Right Words, rwpublish73@gmail.com

This Work is Copyright © Richard Brown 2013

ISBN 978-0-9538721-1-4

Printed by CPI Group (UK) CR0 4YY.

Set in 11/14pt Baskerville

Acknowledgements

So much time, so many people! It would be invidious to attempt to name individuals but to those who, over the decades, have…

- listened
- read
- argued
- tolerated
- encouraged
- recommended
- proselytised
- teased
- tussled
- lauded
- puzzled
- debated
- counselled
- written
- suggested
- compared
- laughed
- sustained
- rejoiced

…I say a profound THANK YOU!

Credits

Design by Clive Batkin
www.clivebatkindesign.co.uk

Editor Anna Reynolds
rwpublish73@gmail.com

Devil's advocacy by Erlend Lee
www.alltimefoundation.com

Cartoon by Joanna Scott
www.joanna-scott.co.uk

Photograph by Donal Corcoran
rwpublish73@gmail.com

Cover texture courtesy of
www.valleysinthevinyl.com

Contents

Something to Believe

This theory depends on acceptance of the laws of logic and a belief that ultimately everything is rationally explicable

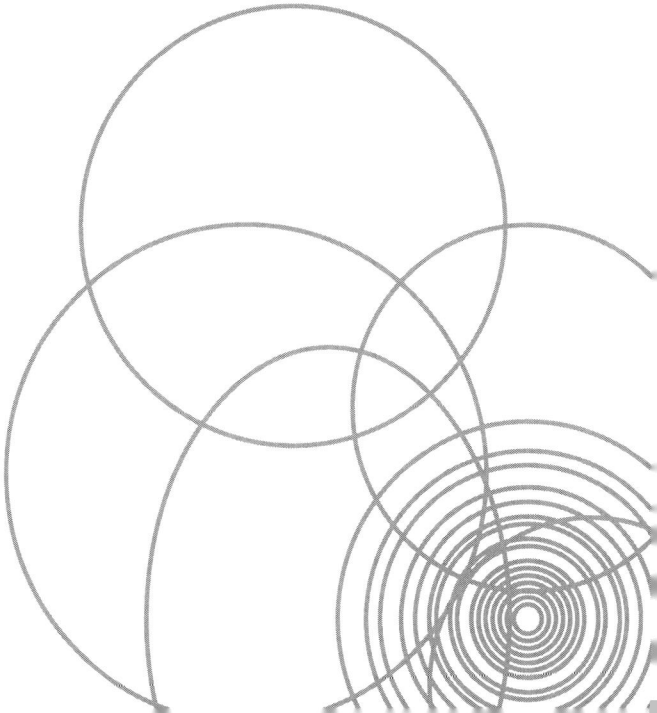

1 ∘ About

*T*his book offers a theory of the universe. Amongst the many questions considered are:

- Where does the universe come from?

- What's the point of our existence?

- Are we machines or are we free?

- Is there life after death?

- How can we stop energy becoming less available?

- What is 'good'?

- Why should we try to be good?

The title promises 'something to believe' and that's what it is.

It's no absolute truth because there's so much we don't yet understand.

It's an attempt to make sense of what we've got so far.

2 ∘ Enough

"We don't need another theory; there are too many as it is."

*I*t's a fair point. There are numerous faith-based accounts and there are other systems which focus on scientific research. Why not just pick one of these?

Here are some reasons for being dissatisfied with what's available.

Religion

This book is not rude about religion. Some of the ideas outlined in the following pages are quite close to some put forward by those who rely on faith. It is probably because core religious beliefs are not far from the truth that they have appealed for so long and to billions of people.

Despite this, though, there are deep problems with religious formulations.

Some of the difficulties are:

o Most religious people claim that their beliefs are the true ones but how are those who don't have a religion to make a choice between all these 'true' accounts which sometimes seem to contradict each other? Even within particular religions there are often differing interpretations.

Why should we go for one rather than another?

o It's probably true that most believers follow the religion of their parents. Does it not seem strange that they just happened to 'land lucky' in the credo lottery?

o Many followers of religion have an 'I know I'm right' attitude but of course anyone can say this about anything. They also say that god gives them faith to believe in him / her. If this is so, why doesn't their god give the same faith to everyone?

o *Where* is god? This is not a silly question and 'everywhere' is not a satisfactory answer.

o If god is as loving and powerful as many believers claim, why is there so much suffering in the world?

Of course, religions have their answers to these questions and to many other challenges but for non-believers they are not very satisfying, especially when all that is offered is 'God's ways are mysterious' or 'You just have to have faith'.

Research
Many take the view that science will eventually provide all the answers. This book is very much in favour of science but it suggests that if scientists want to give us a complete story of the universe there are several problems which strongly challenge the scientific process. Two of these are discussed immediately below, others will emerge later.

Causes

Objects fall, fire heats, planets follow their orbits. Science relies on there being rigid rules governing the universe. Mostly we take them for granted but where do these rules come from?

Mind

Science works by observing things that happen. It's possible to see the workings of a brain but how could we ever directly experience the operation of a human mind other than our own? All that we have is what people tell us about their thoughts and feelings; we can't ever know for sure what it's like to be another person. The inner world is not systematically accessible to science.

Don't know

In the face of these and other difficulties some argue that there's no point in trying to work out what the universe is doing because it's too complicated. Generally such 'agnostics' say that all we can do is live our lives for the best.

There is a problem as to how we can know what is best but 'don't know' would perhaps be a sensible stance if religion and science were the only options.

But there is another way of formulating theories of the universe and its name is metaphysics.

3 ∘ Metaphysics

*M*etaphysics is taken simply to mean 'beyond physics'. This doesn't imply that metaphysics is against science; far from it. What it does allow is that ideas which can't yet be proved can be put together to form a picture.

But it's not like the kind of picture produced by religions. There are no sacred texts delivered by gods, no divine revelations given to gurus. Also there are no priests and institutions to keep people on the 'right' track.

Instead there are ideas produced by human thought, notions which can be constantly questioned and revised as knowledge grows and as thinkers invent new ways of fitting the jigsaw pieces of the universe puzzle together.

So, metaphysical accounts of the universe don't depend on faith and they don't rely totally on research; they are the product of human reason.

This means, of course, that there can be very many different theories. How are we to judge which one is the best for us? Happily there are ways of assessment. Here are some of them:

Coherence
Does the theory 'hold together'? Does it make sense? Do the key concepts have clear meaning?

Simplicity

Is the account free of needless complications?

Logicality

Is the argument devoid of contradictions and other breaches of the laws of logic?

Science

Of course scientists make mistakes and are not always clear. Quite often they have fierce arguments amongst themselves about the best way of expressing things but science has painstakingly built up a body of knowledge which cannot be ignored.

So, a crucial test of a metaphysical theory is to measure how far it agrees with scientific truth. Suppose, for example, that someone sets out to explain things on the assumption that Earth is flat. It would have to be a very powerful theory indeed for it to be acceptable because we know for sure that Earth is approximately spherical.

Explanation

The whole point of creating a theory is to explain things. This is perhaps the most important test of all. If ideas which were separate become satisfyingly linked and if light is shone into some dark corners, then the theory is of value.

Prediction

Metaphysical theories can make predictions. Generally they are ones which will take a very long time to be tested but nonetheless a mark of a good metaphysical theory, just as with a scientific one, is that it can eventually be checked.

4 ∘ Existence

*T*he proposed metaphysical account begins with a definition:

The universe is everything that exists, has existed and will exist

The first obvious question is; where did this 'everything' come from? – a problem which has perplexed thinkers for thousands of years.

It is logically inescapable that any attempt to explain where everything comes from would have to start with nothing. 'Everything' is, by the above definition, all-inclusive.

Yet the great Aristotle said: 'Nothing can come from nothing'.

In this context, 'nothing' does not mean darkness, nor 'empty space'; it means literally 'no thing'. We don't need to try to imagine it because there is nothing to be imagined. The word is a mental off switch.

Surely, therefore, Aristotle was right but in a relatively recent attempt to escape the problem a renowned scientist suggested that the universe came into being through 'an accident happening in nothing'.

How could this be? 'Nothing' is by definition

unimaginable and therefore we could never devise an experiment, neither mental nor physical, to prove the assertion that everything comes from nothing. In any case, what possible meaning could the word 'accident' have in the context of nothingness?

Many other thinkers have accepted Aristotle's assertion that we have no option but to take existence for granted.

One example is Descartes whose famous dictum was; 'I think, therefore I am'. This proposal has considerable difficulties one of which is that the first 'I' presupposes his existence but he could have said 'Thinking, therefore existence' and still made his point that we have to start with something.

Much nearer to our time, Wittgenstein opened his famous Tractatus with; 'The world is all that is the case'. By 'the world' he surely means 'the universe' so he seems to imply that there cannot be something made from nothing.

For the most part, religions try to solve the problems of the origin of existence by citing a god as the instigator of everything but of course a god is a 'thing' so it doesn't help. It is fair to ask theists: 'Where does god come from?'

Many centuries ago there was a thinker called Occam who suggested that we should make explanations as simple as possible. He argued that we shouldn't invent ideas just for the sake of it.

This 'Occam's razor' seems very sensible. If the existence of gods could be proved they would have to be included in the theory but we don't have such a proof. So, instead of saying: 'The universe was made by a god who has always existed', we can just say that overall the universe is timeless. (It is not so within but of that more later).

'Nothing from nothing' doesn't mean that there's nothing to be said about existence. Quite soon some ideas will be explored which will hopefully make it easier to accept that 'the world is all that is the case.'

5 ○ Fundamentals

All very well perhaps but the thing which is being 'taking for granted' involves a hugely complicated array of objects, thoughts and processes. Surely the universe is far too diverse to be described by a single theory. How can the daunting array of stars, planets, people, dreams and all the other paraphernalia be reduced to manageable proportions?

Energy

The first step in the answer offered here is to assert that **everything that is manifest in the universe is the result of the operation of energy**.

This is the universal 'stuff' and is the first of two 'fundamentals' or axioms.

When walking along a street, feet firmly on the pavement, houses to left and right, trees in gardens, it's very difficult indeed to accept that all the things that we can feel, see, hear, taste and smell are composed of tiny bundles of energy; but so they are.

Perhaps it is even harder to acknowledge that we ourselves are just complex arrangements of energy but that's the truth.

Just as it is very tempting to ask where everything comes from so there is a strong drive to ask what energy is made of.

The answer is that energy is not made of anything; it just is.

We can best call it an 'abstraction'. There are zillions upon zillions of manifestations of energy and our abstract idea of it comes from this vast variety.

Energy can be defined as 'the essence of everything'.

But energy is not quite all because the stuff has to be somewhere.

Space

Obviously, it is in space.

This is the second of the fundamentals. Like energy, space is not made from anything and it is also an abstraction.

In fact, **space can be defined as 'the absence of everything'**

But this does not mean that it is nothing. As noted above, nothing is 'no thing' whereas space is very definitely a 'thing'.

A 20th century philosopher called Strawson bravely tried to imagine and describe a 'no space' universe but his effort wasn't convincing.

Since 'nothing' is unthinkable it must be the case that there is no energy without space and no space without energy. This theoretical conclusion is backed by recent scientific developments which strongly suggest that the universe is pervaded by something called 'dark energy.'

wo fundamentals are evidently interdependent and it seems clear that the simplest description of the universe is that it is **'a system of energy operating in space'**.

Time

Emerging from these two fundamental concepts is their 'child'; time.

Time comes about because energy has two ways of manifesting itself, the continuous (waveform) and the discontinuous (particle).

If all energy were continuous there could be no time. Time depends on division. It can be defined as **'the most general expression of the operation of discontinuous energy in space'**.

Like its parents, time is not made from anything and is thus also an abstraction.

So, energy / space / time is the fundamental trinity of existence.

As an interesting aside, it is here noted that each of these basic entities generates its own characteristic subsidiary trinity.

Energy has positive / negative / neutral.

Space has three dimensions of equal stature.

Time has past / present / future.

Small wonder perhaps that 'three-ness' shows up so frequently in religious and other thought systems.

6 ∘ Infinity

*T*hus the purpose of this book is to provide a general account of the system of energy operating in space.

However, despite the energy / space / time simplification, there is a potential problem with size.

Many people believe that the universe is infinite; how can any theory encompass infinity?

'Infinite' is often used to mean 'very far' or 'very many' but it is taken here to mean 'without limit'.

If it were a real thing, infinity would indeed make the generation of a satisfactory theory impossible but happily it doesn't need to be considered because the word 'infinite' refers to nothing real.

For infinity to be real it would be necessary;

o to be able to imagine it and / or

o to prove its existence physically.

But how could we ever imagine boundlessness? What we can imagine is something being indefinite but this is not infinity. By its very definition infinity cannot be contained; no satisfactory concept can be formed.

And neither could we ever physically 'prove' infinity.

Suppose we send out a superfast probe on a straight

trajectory. If the universe is 'infinite' the probe's journey would never reach a conclusion. At what point would we be able to declare 'Ah! Infinity'? For all we would know, the probe might eventually hit a containing wall.

Many people speak as though infinity is a place. 'Parallel lines meet at infinity' is a common example. If 'parallel' lines meet they are not parallel and there can be no 'at infinity'.

Because infinity is impossible it must be inevitably concluded that the universe is finite.

But if this is so, what's outside it?

Because the universe has been defined as 'all existence' there can be only one logical answer to the 'what's outside?' question and it is: *Nothing*. There *is* no 'outside'.

But what can it mean to say that there's no outside?

Again, there is but one allowable answer: We are irrevocably inside the ball of energy.

But how could the universe be like this? What is there to stop us getting 'out'?

7 ○ Containment

*O*ne suggestion is that space is somehow curved to form a peculiar kind of surface. Of course, gravity causes the trajectories of objects travelling through the cosmos to bend but this is not the same as a curvature of space itself.

It is difficult to imagine how something without structure and parts (ie space) could be shaped but if indeed we do exist on a mysterious imaginary surface then it would imply that, just as we can go into the interior of our planet and also fly above it, so should we be able to:

- ○ go below the supposed space surface (akin to going down a mineshaft) and

- ○ go above this surface (akin to taking off in an aeroplane) into what some call 'hyperspace'.

But it doesn't seem we can do these things. Rather than being on a curved surface we are fairly obviously in a three-dimensional medium in which we can potentially move at will.

Yet further, there is strong scientific evidence based on temperature measurements that space is not curved.

But if we are to escape the infinity puzzle, the universe must be somehow circumscribed.

How?

The argument in response to this is as follows.

o It has been proposed that at the ultimate level of analysis we have only energy and space.

o It is also the case that space is not the agent of containment.

o Therefore the containing agent must be energy.

8 ○ *Energy*

*M*odern science tells us that there are two categories of energy; the 'light', which we can perceive and the 'dark', which until the very recent discovery of the elusive Higgs boson has been known only by inference. The existence of the Higgs particle more or less confirms that dark energy makes up about 70% of the universe's stock.

Perceivable energy

In Ancient Greece, philosophers were attracted by the idea that everything is made of one thing. Some suggestions were earth, air, fire and water but one thinker, Democritus, put forward an 'atomic theory' which held that everything is made of atoms arranged in different ways.

For a long time it has been generally agreed that some kind of atomic theory is essentially true but we now think of atoms as consisting of even smaller units such as electrons, protons and the like.

Scientists tell us that the arrangement of the particles is very similar to the way in which the sun and planets are organised. Each atom has a central bit called a 'nucleus' which has other bits whizzing round them. Some of the bits exist only for astonishingly small amounts of time before changing into some other manifestation of energy.

It would surely be very convenient for researchers if these 'quantum particles' were always like hard pellets but they're not. The extraordinary thing is that sometimes they behave as if they were 'solid' but at others they seem to be like packets of waves.

This puzzle was first noticed in connection with light which sometimes seems to be a continuous wave and sometimes a stream of particles. The mystery appeared to be unsolvable and one scientist jokingly suggested that we should use the particle theory on three days of the week, the wave theory on another three with Sunday off.

Scientists have long experimented and argued. They wanted to explain how one thing, an electron for example, could be both 'hard' and 'soft' at the same time. How can something be simultaneously concentrated and spread out?

This is very peculiar but there's another oddity which goes against a simple account.

All of science is based upon the idea that things are made to happen; the football goes towards the goal because it has been kicked. But it seems that some of the movements of the particles happen without anything making them happen. Electrons hop from one orbit to another for no obvious reason.

And there's more!

The tiny 'quantum particles' are not only capable of being both hard and soft, and of moving without apparently being pushed or pulled, they can seemingly do some other astonishing tricks.

Here are three examples:

o Particles which are in the wave form will turn into the hard form only if they are observed by a conscious being or by an instrument introduced by a person.

o Sometimes particles can instantly communicate with each other even if they are far apart.

o Particles can instantaneously 'jump' vast distances.

These amazing attributes are called 'quantum properties'.

The great Einstein didn't like quantum properties one little bit and called them 'spooky interactions'. He also didn't welcome the idea that the particles can move without being forced. He firmly believed that everything in nature is made to happen. He said, 'God does not play dice.'

Despite the great man's opposition, it is now very widely accepted that quantum particles do have weird properties and that they do move as though 'of their own free will'. Later, an explanation will be offered as to how this might be.

Dark energy

Of its mysterious nature very little is known about dark energy. Later a proposal will be made as to what might be its function but for the time being it is assumed that one or both of the two types of energy set the universal limits.

How it might be

So, to add at least a little substance to what might seem a nebulous conception, imagine travelling in a rocket ship, hurtling away from Earth at a speed which currently seems impossible. All around are vast arrays of stars, planets, moons, comets. Let's suppose that you are in some life-preserving coma state but that every now and then you wake up to find out where you are.

Whenever you check, you confirm that you are going as straight as you can but to your amazement you discover that, after a very long travel indeed, galaxies which were behind you as you set off have appeared in front. All the ones around you seem to have changed position too. Bravely you keep going and going until you realise that our own galaxy, which of course you expect to be behind you, is actually dead ahead

This seems impossible but suppose you were on a flat, featureless beach of indefinite extension. In the middle of a dense patch of fog you start to walk to get out of the cloud but there's a gentle current of air somehow linked to you which makes the fog drift such that every time you move, the fog moves with you. Whichever way you turn you stay in the middle.

The case with the universe has to be very different but instead of thinking of it as a blank three-dimensional canvas imagine a massive mist of quantum particles and dark energy all of which can do amazing things.

There is no doubt that this suggestion of constant adjustment is a bold one but it is clear that the ways of the universe are mysterious to an extraordinary degree. Indeed, some scientists who study the cosmos claim that everything appears to be simultaneously in the centre.

It may of course be that there is some other explanation as to how we are enclosed in the mist of energy but it seems fairly sure that we are.

This, of course, fits with the earlier claim that the account of energy must be a circular one.

But if circularity is true, it brings us to a major difficulty, one that is called 'entropy'.

9 ∘ Entropy

*A*ll the indications are that the availability of energy is very gradually decreasing. Suns are burning out, the universe is becoming colder and colder.

This is 'entropy'; the increasing unavailability of energy.

Some scientists predict that the universe will end in a 'soup' which will be at absolute-zero temperature. Oddly, some say that this would involve an increase in chaos but obviously, as activity dwindled, things would actually become ever slower and simpler – the opposite of chaos.

This final countdown cannot happen because the notion of energy utterly implies activity. If all activity ceased, the so-called 'primal soup' could only be nothing but we know that something cannot become nothing.

If energy were simply and only physical in manifestation, entropy would seem to be an unsolvable problem but unsurprisingly things are a great deal more subtle.

10 ∘ *Willpower*

*W*e experience the operation of energy in two ways. There is an 'outer' (objective) world of things such as trees, tables, forces, water and so on and on and there is an 'inner' (subjective) world of perceptions, emotions, ideas and dreams.

One of the hardest problems in philosophy concerns the relationship between these two worlds.

Some claim that the world of 'things' is primary and that conscious beings such as ourselves are just some more things that the objective world happens to have produced.

Others are of the opinion that the inner world is primary and that we 'construct' the outer world from the mental data. Some go so far as to claim that 'things' pop out of existence whenever they are unperceived.

Both of these approaches pose problems. For example:

- ∘ If the physical world is primary, how, when and why did consciousness evolve?

- ∘ It seems self-contradictory to speak of 'things' which exist only when perceived. In what sense can a supposed non-existent entity be a 'thing'?

- ∘ If things pop in and out of existence depending

on whether or not they are perceived how do they do so with such reliability? Surely, with a nod towards Occam, 'continuous existence' is the most economical theory.

Many proponents of the objective approach believe that one day science will 'explain' consciousness. They claim that once the physical operation of the brain is fully understood it will be possible to 'read' what someone is thinking.

Indeed there will surely be very many correlations between brain events and reported thought processes but no matter how knowledgeable we become there can be no objective access to the subjective world; the two realms are inescapably separate.

This observation leads to an important metaphysical proposal which is justified because;

a it resolves the problem of the relationship between the 'inner' and the 'outer' and

b it helps massively in the formation of a theory which deals with entropy.

The proposal is that;

a   all manifestations of energy have 'inner' and 'outer' aspects.

b the two aspects are 'associated' and not causally linked; that is, they are like two sides of one coin.

The proposition is that all manifestations of energy, however simple, have a subjective aspect.

The idea that objects are not totally inanimate is an ancient one. Some form of 'animism' has been believed by, at the very least, millions. Even in supposedly sophisticated modern times people frequently assign genders and personalities to well-loved machines such as cars and boats. It is very evident, though, that some entities (humans for example) have much more inner activity than do others (eg rocks). What governs the relative levels?

It seems reasonable to suggest that the ratio between the objective and subjective aspects for any entity is related to two factors, namely;

a the complexity and

b the dynamism of that entity.

Thus a spade (simple and with no moving parts) has a near negligible 'inner' aspect whereas a tiger (much more complex and with significant internal movement) has very considerably more.

The crucial relevance in relation to entropy is that with consciousness comes willpower.

We experience willpower directly; it is self-generated.

It is here proposed that **it is willpower which will reverse entropy.**

Thus a crucial prediction of the theory is that a brain which is involved in a thinking process will cause a net increase in energy, though this may be mediated through the dark variety which of course will make it extremely difficult to detect.

11 ∘ *Structure*

*T*he proposal is that as the universe evolves, **complexity and dynamism will hugely increase.**

From the current position, where the physical aspect of energy vastly predominates, the doubtless multifarious peoples of the universe will create ever more consciousness.

As they do so it is inevitable that the present physical expansion of energy will be reversed. Complexity will entail a coming together. Eventually the organisation will reach an optimum state where consciousness, and hence willpower, are at maximum. Conversely, physicality will be at a minimum.

For the purposes of this theory this 'end point' can be called **'Omega'.**

It has already been noted that the story of energy has to be circular. It follows then that if Omega is to exist in the future it must have also existed in the past.

There is powerful evidence that it did. It seems as near certain as can be that something over fourteen billion years ago all of the energy in the universe was concentrated into one entity which is sometimes called the 'primal atom'.

This 'start point' is here called **'Alpha'**.

We know also that the primal atom blew up.

The explosion fragmented energy, converting it instantly from maximum mentality to maximum physicality and sending it rushing outwards at fantastic speed. This initiated a phase of the universe, of which we are all a tiny part, which can be called **'Nature'**.

It is proposed that the task of Nature is to bring us to a point where we can reintegrate energy.

For the circle to be complete, the Alpha and Omega states have to be identical in every respect. They can therefore have the same name, let's say 'Alphoma'.

Thus the circle is:

Alphoma - explosion - Nature - reintegration - Alphoma

It is crucial to the theory that this is seen as a structure as well as a process.

For excellent reasons of survival in the mayhem of Nature we are very strongly 'conditioned' to think in a linear fashion. Because of this, structural thinking is difficult at first.

Perhaps the strongest incentive to persist with a structural approach is the recognition that a linear account is logically impossible. To repeat, in the form of a mantra; something cannot come from nothing and cannot become nothing. Compared to dealing with these 'impossibles' the effort of cultivating an alternative interpretation is slight.

Obviously we need to continue to think linearly when appropriate; the two methods are complementary not competitive.

For Nature to succeed in reintegration there must be a mental force equivalent to gravity.

This force must;

o be intrinsically attractive (in the sense of pulling things together)

o work towards the elimination of conflict (otherwise total reintegration of energy will not be possible) and

o be maximally desirable.

Of course there is such a force and we call it 'love'.

The level of love in the universe will spasmodically increase as we work towards Omega.

This implies that **Alphoma is a place of bliss.**

But if life is so idyllic in Alphoma why do the denizens destroy it?

They do so because they must.

12 ∘ Nature

The explosion happens because Alphomans need to generate consciousness, for without willpower the energy cycle cannot be completed.

But the big bang cannot be an uncontrolled event. If there were no constraints there could be no guaranteed circle and thus no existence.

This formulation resolves the ancient debate about whether the universe is machine-like (ie 'determined') or free; it is both.

It is suggested that there are at least two ways in which the Alphomans design the guidance of the Nature phase;

Forces

They set up a system of immutable forces of which the most obvious is gravity, There are of course other natural forces which keep things under a measure of control but gravity is very obviously 'trying' to pull everything back together.

Nudges

The proposed 'nudges' allow freedom but come into play to maintain an overall 'steer'.

The most evident example of this is associated with the 'survival of the fittest' mechanism which helps hugely to ensure that Nature works towards the development of consciousness. This evolutionary process depends on genetic mutation which is often said to occur 'at random'.

Usually 'at random' is taken to mean 'without cause'. Einstein repudiated the notion of things occurring spontaneously and surely he was right to do so. Devices such as roulette wheels, which are generally thought to be sources of randomness, could in fact be totally predicted if someone had the time, knowledge and instruments to work out the physics.

Science is entirely dependent on causation and the only true randomness is that generated via the exercise of will.

The radical suggestion is that dark energy is a vast computer-like device which pervades the entire universe. It is programmed by the Alphomans to guarantee the deterministic forces of Nature. It also has sensors which keep an overall check on the effects of free will. It is not a deity, it does not judge nor offer rewards and punishments nor issue revelations, it allows freedom but steers when necessary to ensure that the goal of Omega is reached.

For there to be choices of real import there have to be 'opposites'; creation/destruction, happiness/sadness and so forth hence, alas, the presence of pain and misery in Nature.

These opposites give meaning to the processes of Nature which is like a river contained by totally secure banks. We individuals are tiny, fleeting droplets with only partial control of our movements but all contributing to the overall flow.

A further pair of speculative proposals about the 'guidance' of Nature concern information.

In Alphoma everything is known. At the big bang all is distributed but it is suggested that each of the fragments from the blast holds bits of information.

Just how this is done, if at all, remains to be seen but it seems that there is plenty of storage capacity in Nature. A recent discovery is that one gram of DNA can store up to 455 billion gigabytes of information. This is the equivalent of more than 100 million DVDs.

If it is true that all information is stored then when we 'wrack our brains' we are perhaps trying to fit pieces together and when Plato claimed that all learning is remembering he was very likely not far from the truth.

As Nature proceeds, the pieces are fitted together such that gradually the original pattern becomes discernible. Through the 'nudges' some individuals have more accessible information than do others which possibly accounts for variations in inventiveness and creativity.

The second proposal about information is that whenever energy is organised by a conscious being it is permanently enhanced even if the organisation is subsequently destroyed. For example, the energy of the shards of a shattered piece of pottery could be subtly different from that in the original clay. Probably, recording of every event, however tiny, is constantly happening.

If this is so then the improved energy will almost certainly be more amenable when it is next used by a conscious being.

Establishing this as a reality, if indeed it is one, will doubtless happen far into the future.

More certain is that, as suggested above, the Alphomans use the controlling devices of laws and nudges to create the conditions for Nature. They understand that it has 'already happened' but they know that, because the universal process is circular, their actions are crucially causative.

For us this is tricky to conceptualise but a development of the river analogy might help. So, imagine that you are, *per impossibile*, outside the universe looking in.

Think of Alphoma as a vast placid lake. At one end is a sluice which releases a turbulent torrent which then forms a raging river within high banks. The river very gradually calms to almost total tranquillity as it is ever more gently pumped upwards to replenish the lake at the opposite end to the sluice.

We are tiny drops in the river, our time fleeting. Although we have considerable free will we often have very limited power against the slings and arrows of fortune. Some are more fortunate than others. On the universal scale of time we exist so briefly.

This is our lot in Nature, in which we inevitably die… so what's the point?

13 ∘ Revival

The point is that as Omega approaches, our successors will work towards the revival of all previously existing entities.

It is a near certainty that there are others in the universe. These, having been through an evolutionary process similar to our own, will be essentially human despite the possibility that they might not look like us. We should think of them as kindred spirits and not as aliens.

There may of course be conflict but all of us, having delved so deep and come to understand the workings of the universe, will agree that only through cooperation can we engineer the route to Omega.

We will be **able** to do this because;

∘ we will have total control over energy and

∘ we will have a complete map of history.

It might be argued that because free will is part of the universal process then a complete map is impossible but this is not so. Events generated by free acts will indeed seem, from the scientific viewpoint, to be 'random' but all events, however caused, have deterministic consequences and can thus be mapped.

We will **want** to revive everyone because:

- we will need to maximise consciousness to generate energy

- we will be motivated by love to want to involve every being in the bliss of Alphoma

- the reintegrated universe will very likely have to include everything.

What will revival be like?

Obviously when we die all sense of time ceases. Thus the first point is that revival will seem to be instant.

The second consideration is that Alphoma is a place of total love. Very few, if any, of us will be in a fit state to slot straight into it; most of us have considerable imperfections.

It might be suggested that in the revival process instant changes could be made but if this were to happen we would not be the same people as we had been. We will have to go through a transition.

Because love is predominant this will not be punitive. Very likely, given the lure of imminent bliss, it will be very short lived.

There is of course a psychological problem relating to the revival of very bad people; the lust for revenge is very powerful within many of us. Some will also suggest that a changed Pol Pot or Hitler would not 'be the same person' after transition but all of us have the potential for creativity and destruction. Radical reforms occur even in Nature. There is always the potential for enlightened change.

14 ∘ *Alphoma*

As Omega approaches we will understand that the time-based Nature phase of the universe is coming to its end. We will know also that once the 'folding in' to Alphoma has happened we will 'resume' our blissful lives. As with our natural death there will be no sense of an interval, our Alphoman lives are effectively 'virtual', free of physical time.

We will see the universe as a structure. We will understand that although almost all the energy in Alphoma is devoted to consciousness there is a residual basis of physicality which, doubtless amongst other things, provides the detonator for the explosion.

All of Nature will be available to us, as will all experiences.

15 ○ Rules

*M*any of the faith-based systems of belief have god-given rules of behaviour. Usually they incorporate a regime of punishments for those who stray. Often something called 'evil' is part of the picture with a personification in the form of a devil or devils.

At the other extreme, a purely scientific account could have nothing to do with morality at all. If everything is 'determined' then there can be no personal responsibility. This exonerates everybody no matter how heinous the sins.

The theory expounded in this book holds that

○ we have a degree of free will and

○ we are working towards a long term goal.

It is surely sensible, therefore, to generate some rules as to how we can best make use of our freedom. The argument runs as follows:

a The fundamental principle (axiom) is that all beings seek to maximise fulfilment.

b Alphoma is a state of maximum fulfilment.

c It therefore follows that we should strive to act in such ways as to bring about the reintegration at Omega.

It is suggested that for this integration to take place we will need to fulfil two conditions.

Firstly we will need to know the truth about everything.

'Truth' is defined as the measure of the degree of correspondence between a state of affairs and a representation of that state of affairs. For example, a painting depicts a view or a person's face and we can judge how 'true' the image is.

Under this definition, truth is a relative term. There can thus be degrees of truth.

Secondly if all humans are to come together at the Omega point we must maximise the force that brings us together, namely **love**.

The rule, therefore, is that as far as possible **we should aim to lead truthful and loving lives**.

Of course, there are lots of different kinds of love. It is not suggested that we have to fall into a romantic state. What it does mean is that we should do as much as we reasonably can to increase the level of human fulfilment.

It might seem from this that we should aim to lead lives of self-sacrifice but if we are to be of use in the struggle towards Omega we need, of course, to survive. And to survive we need to have at least some of our needs met.

In life we are frequently faced with a conflict between

our desire for personal gratification and a belief that we should help others. Do we have a holiday or make a contribution to famine relief? Evidently we need to find a balance which is perhaps best encapsulated in the 'love thy neighbour as thyself' precept.

It is perhaps worth noting that there cannot be an absolute unselfishness. Even if we choose to suffer on behalf of others, or in order to satisfy a god, we are doing what we decide to do and thus satisfy ourselves.

Short-termism
The big bang sets up opposites; light / dark, love / hatred, positive / negative, creation/destruction. Without these there could be no meaning and no opportunity to generate the essential will-power. Negativity is thus an inescapable part of the universal process.

Until Omega is reached, individuals therefore have the freedom to choose to disdain the truth and to act un-lovingly.

It might be asked; if everyone is to be welcomed into Alphoma, why should people not grab all they can in life regardless of the needs of others?

There are two inducements to follow the rule:

Transition
There can be no badness in Alphoma. It is a place of total love. Those whose life in Nature is not based on love will have to go through a process of transition between the moment of revival and reception into Omega.

There will be nothing deliberately punitive about this transition but it will inevitably involve some painful adjustment.

The more we can do during our lives to become loving and truthful beings the easier will be the process of transition.

Fulfilment now

A prediction is that people who live loving and truthful lives will, in general, be more fulfilled in the Nature phase of their existence than those who ignore the fundamental precepts.

Rights

It is often suggested that there are such things as absolute rights. This stance implies that there is an agency which decides the list of entitlements. In this theory the only source of rights is human invention.

On Earth, despite the terrible deeds of some, there is happily a broad consensus in favour of the promotion of human freedom and the pursuit of happiness.

This is doubtless because enough of us intuit the primacy of truth and love. There could, however, be entire planets where, temporarily at least, terror reigns and, of course, it could happen here.

If there are or will be such places, part of the process towards Omega will be to overcome hatred and cruelty and to persuade the negative ones that their ways are counter-productive.

Dealing with rule-breakers

Whether on this cosmic scale or here on Earth it is open for humankind to make rules. How should we deal with those who offend against the generally agreed standards?

Justice

Justice can be construed as a combination of truth and love. The injunction to act in the spirit of these two values applies just as much to the treatment of malefactors as it does in all other circumstances.

Punishment

We can never know the mind of another person. For this reason we have to avoid making assumptions about moral responsibility.

It is probably quite rare for someone to think: "I believe this act is wrong but I'm still going to do it". Usually there are circumstances which cause people to behave unthinkingly or there is a rationale which makes the behaviour seem acceptable to the perpetrator.

If someone feels guilty about something they have done then they punish themselves. If they don't feel guilty, anything which society does to them feels like nothing other than a form of torture.

There is thus no need to build punishment into the system. Our response to wrongdoing needs to be pragmatic as suggested in the next three sections.

Protection

The primary purpose of taking action against those

who break the democratically agreed rules of society is to protect others. This will sometimes involve the incarceration of criminals but not their execution which, of course, takes away any prospect of reform.

Reparation

A major aspect of the response to wrongdoing should be the offering of opportunities to make reparation to those who have been harmed by the destructive acts.

Education

A further aspect is the offering of opportunities for education such that wrongdoers might come to accept the love / truth imperative and also learn skills which will improve their prospects of making a positive contribution to the development of society.

Love / truth conflicts

Of course there are many instances in life when love and truth come into conflict. Sometimes it seems that the most loving act is to tell a lie.

In these circumstances love takes priority; the truth will eventually emerge even if only at the Omega point. Love is the imperative. It is the mental equivalent of gravity which will make total unity an inevitable outcome.

16 ○ *Supernature*

*S*ome people maintain that there are hauntings, thought-transference, psycho-kinesis and other mysterious happenings which seem to be beyond the usual processes of scientific investigation. These events are often called 'paranormal' or 'supernatural'.

Many scientists are interested only in events which can be reliably repeated and so they tend to reject these scientifically dubious occurrences. This is fine as a declaration of policy but it is wrong to put all the non-replicable occurrences into the 'unreal' bin. Belief in the supernatural is very widespread. Very many 'sober citizens' have had powerful experiences which are difficult to explain. It could be that it takes relatively rare combinations of subtle factors for 'supernatural' events to take place. It could also be that the very process of objective research inhibits the appearance of the phenomena.

A very common way of accounting for the so-called supernatural is to suggest that there are entities such as spirits, angels and ghosts which exist independently beyond the realm of the physical.

This formulation does not suit this theory because of the crucial claim that all manifestations of energy have physical and mental aspects.

This chapter presents some suggested explanations of what might be called 'subtle phenomena'. The range of these is very wide but listed below are some general assumptions which underpin the accounts.

Ground rules

1   The brain is an electrical device with a force field which extends beyond the head.

2   Dark energy pervades the universe. Probably, many esoteric phenomena involve interaction between our brains and dark energy which makes the physical aspect very difficult to detect.

3   Quanta can interact instantaneously at great distances.

4   The forces involved in subliminal interactions are generally weak.

5   Because physical survival has been, and still is, the absolute imperative it is probable that modern humans have adapted to pay maximum attention to information conveyed by the senses and to pay minimum attention to subliminal data. (From the survival point of view, it's more important to see traffic as we cross a road than to pick up the ideas or feelings being broadcast by another mind).

6   It might be, therefore, that some of our ancestors were better adapted for subtle interactions but that they did not fare well in the evolutionary struggle.

7   Probably the optimum conditions for modern humans to experience subtle events involve a strong signal (eg one associated with great joy or trauma) and mentally 'quiet' conditions for the recipient.

8   Probably there is something about 'being on the same wavelength' which is not yet reliably in our control.

9   It is at least possible that our environment records data, albeit in weak form, just as audio / video tapes and discs do. So, for example, the energy making up the walls of a room which is the location for a dramatic event is probably slightly but permanently changed by that event.

10 It is at least possible that energy is also permanently altered by being part of an organisation.

11 As noted earlier, it could also be that we have access to subliminal sources of data.

Explanations / ideas

1   Soul

It is quite commonly assumed that a human acquires a soul at birth and loses it at death. This raises awkward questions as to what souls are made of, where they come from and where they go.

Rather than think in terms of entities of uncertain structure and movement this theory, as already noted, prefers the notion that the amount of mental activity is proportional to;

- o the complexity of the arrangement of energy and

- o the degree to which the arrangement is working.

Human beings are very complex and very vigorous; the level of mental activity is relatively high. When someone dies, the 'working' aspect ceases; mental activity drops dramatically but, it is suggested, there is no 'floating off' of ectoplasm. Eventually the physical form is dispersed, thus removing even the element of organisation.

2   Near death experiences

Some people who have been very close to death and have then recovered claim to have had unusual experiences. Quite often they enjoy great peace but they also receive a 'message' to the effect that there is more yet for them to do.

Alphoma does not actually exist during the Nature phase of the universe so how can there be any inkling of a life beyond the one we know?

The proposed answer is that for some people the approach to death brings about a filtering out of the 'noise' of our environment. In such conditions, receptivity to subtle sources of information is at a maximum.

This heightened awareness allows a 'logging in' to otherwise inaccessible stored data. The person close to death perceives an imprecise but nonetheless powerful intimation of the future bliss. But for 'near death' people this glimpse of the truth also shows that death is actually not imminent. The interpretation of this information as a 'message' is entirely understandable.

3 Mystics

For time immemorial there have been people of a very wide variety of creeds and cultures, who, wittingly or otherwise, have attempted to create near-death conditions. Known as mystics, they have isolated and starved themselves in order to minimise the impact of the physical aspect of energy. It is here suggested that their experiences are explicable in very much the same way as the near death ones.

Regardless of their religious persuasions and cultural influences mystics generally report that the end point of the universe is a state of bliss in which every one of us, unified by love, has god-like powers.

4 Extra-sensory perception / Thought transference

Sometimes we seem to hear or see events which are beyond the normal range of our senses. It is also sometimes claimed that thoughts can be beamed directly from one mind to another.

Probably this is simply a weak 'broadcast and receive' phenomenon which perhaps works all the time at a subliminal level but which, due to ambient 'noise', rarely comes to consciousness.

There is some evidence that animals, generally unencumbered by intellectual 'noise', can 'sense' things at a subliminal level. It is also sometimes claimed that some of our gentler ancestors made use of thought-transference.

As we evolve and the survival stresses diminish we will surely rediscover the skills of physically unaided communication at a distance.

5   Apparitions

Very likely, 'ghosts' are 'record and playback' phenomena. Particularly dramatic occurrences doubtless become more imprinted on the immediate environment than do less vigorous events. For the most part, the recorded message is not strong enough for us to access and most of us are far too preoccupied to be sufficiently receptive. Sometimes, though, a highly sensitive person who just happens to be 'tuned' to the right frequency, seems to pick up such recorded data.

6   Psychokinesis

There have been many attempts to show that humans can move or shape things purely by the power of thought but there is no definitive laboratory evidence. As noted earlier, it is entirely possible that the objective set-up of experiments inhibits the very process under investigation. However there is much anecdotal material which suggests that we can sometimes 'make things happen'.

If this is a real phenomenon then it must be that, under optimum conditions, the energy broadcast from the brain can interact significantly with the energy of objects.

7   Poltergeists

A very extreme form of psychokinesis is the oft-reported violent movement of objects. Generally this is associated with people who are enduring great mental turbulence. Presumably their heightened energy provides the power and it is also likely that the inhibitory factors which generally provide us with control are, in connection with this phenomenon, much weakened or even disabled.

8   Dowsing

Some forms of dowsing, a technique used, amongst many other things, to locate underground water or objects, seem to combine extra-sensory perception and psycho-kinesis.

9   Faith healing

There seems to be no definitive evidence that something like faith healing is efficacious but this is another idea which pervades and persists. Many people are convinced that they can influence their own healing by thinking positively. And it has been shown, for example, that patients who have beautiful scenery outside their hospital windows recover faster than those with nothing pleasant to behold. Further evidence of mind-body interaction is provided by the apparent efficacy of placebos.

It could be that, like other mental phenomena, the forces behind faith healing are too sporadic and weak to make experimental proof possible. The prediction is that it will eventually become apparent that healing can be accelerated both by a positive attitude on the part of the sick person and by mental input from others.

As with the other subtle phenomena, there is nothing unscientific about this. The probability is that the extremely powerful anti-viral and anti-bacterial mechanisms in the body are inhibited by stress and by a lack of positive attitude. If this is so, all that self-healing involves is the mental effort to relax as much as possible, to focus on the perceived site of the ailment and to encourage the body to fight off the viral or bacteriological invader.

Where others are involved, as in the laying on of hands or through a form of prayer, there are, no doubt, real forces passing from the healer to the invalid. Probably almost any human can help any other one in this way but it is fairly sure that disbelief in the possibility will act as an 'off' switch.

Whilst necessarily keeping an open mind on the matter, it would seem that there is enough evidence to take the risk-free gamble of believing in 'faith healing'. The important caveat, however, is that the faith is not in a god but in ourselves.

10 Mental disturbance

It might seem inappropriate to include mental disturbance in this review of subtle phenomena but it is here argued that, at least in some cases, what appears to be irrational behaviour is in fact a response to the reception by the afflicted person of difficult-to-explain data.

If the proposal of the subtlety of information transfer is correct then it is not surprising that sensitive people sometimes 'hear voices' and have unbidden thoughts. We should perhaps be slower to make diagnostic judgements and more patient in the interpretation of 'insanity'.

17 ∘ Questions

*T*he universe is expanding. Even if it turns out to be true that we can never get out of the ball of energy, surely it could go on expanding for ever. Are we not still stuck with the possibility of infinity?

It's a matter of inescapable physical fact that the expansion will eventually come to an end. Either, as many believe, energy will just run out or there will, as proposed by this theory, be an organised contraction. Either way there's no meaning to 'infinity'.

Linear thinking has been so successful; is it not just a matter of time before it provides all the answers?

It's easy to be overawed by the success of science. The evidence of achievement, in the guise of explanations, amazing devices and mystifying mathematics, is inescapable. But all in the scientific garden is not perfect. Some examples of disarray are:

o Relativity theory and quantum mechanics have yet to be reconciled.

o There are fundamental problems with infinity, causation, entropy and the mind-body relationship.

- o In what seems like desperation, some scientists argue that there is 'an infinite number' of 'parallel universes'. 'Infinite number' is meaningless and for these mysterious 'other universes' there appears to be no empirical evidence at all.

- o Similarly it is suggested that there are 'other dimensions' some of which are 'folded small' to a degree where we will never be able to perceive them. Can this be good science?

In short, science does not have all the answers and, as argued, will never do so. The difficulties associated with structural thinking have to be seen in this context of the drawbacks with the linear approach.

Can anything be done to make circularity easier to accept?

We can be relentless with Aristotle's logic; nothing can come from nothing. We can agree that we are conditioned to think in straight lines because that is what has ensured our survival. It usually seems like the only way but it can't be.

It's maybe worth noting also that roundness appears to be a major feature of the universe. Most of the objects in space are roughly spherical. It has just been shown that electrons are almost perfectly so as is our sun. Heavenly bodies move in orbits. It is surely not too preposterous to assume that the whole thing is ball-like.

Perhaps, above all, we can acknowledge the explanatory power of the circular account.

Circularity suggests that everything has 'already happened' so why are we struggling along?
This is a question rooted in linear thinking. As hitherto suggested, we need to try to think of the history of the universe as a structure. Our successors create Alphoma and incorporate the time bomb which brings about the big bang. They manage things so that after the explosion there is overall certainty that the circle will be completed but, because there is free will, the details of the route taken from Alpha to Omega are not predictable. The intricacies of that section can be ascertained only by research after the events have happened.

All of history is in Alphoma but all that we have, in the Nature phase, are the fragments of the whole picture. Through our choices we create that picture. In fact we create ourselves and we will see the universal picture in its entirety only when the primal atom is put back together.

What does it mean to claim that the only truly random events come about by the operation of will?
Some scientists hold that there are sub-atomic events which happen 'spontaneously', that is, without cause.

The theory expounded in this book proposes that there are two types of causes, the physical and the mental.

It is suggested that most if not all of the events normally called 'random' are physically caused via the operation of dark energy.

It is predicted that some brain events associated with

thinking will seem, from the objective point of view, to be spontaneous. Thus a conscious being can invent, for example, a series of numbers which to an observer of the brain will be unpredictable. By contrast, any 'objective' generation of a number sequence is potentially predictable.

What would happen if the Omega Project went wrong?

It can't. We know this because we exist. If the principle of the universe were destructive there could be no circle.

Could there be other universes?

This theory is based on the definition that the universe is everything that has existence so the obvious logical answer is there cannot be other universes.

If there are other closed systems like ours then we will either eventually link with them or we will not. If we do then they will be part of the universe and will have to be somehow incorporated into the overall theory. If not, they can be no concern of ours.

Could there be more than one universal cycle?

In other words, could the unified state which we create at the Omega point explode differently, setting up an entirely new passage of Nature?

At Omega we are in total control of the universe. Our Alphoman lives will be perfect. Why would we want to destroy ourselves?

Does the theory depend on there being other self-conscious creatures in the universe?
Logically speaking, no. In theory, Earth could be the one place in the universe where consciousness has evolved to a high level. If this is so then we must conclude that all future development will stem from us.

So, there is no absolute dependence but with the billions upon billions of other possible venues for consciousness development it seems near certain that we are not alone.

If there are other human-like creatures in the universe, why have they not made contact?
Maybe, like us, they don't yet know how to or perhaps they know that it's best, at this stage of our development, not to interfere.

Could Earthly civilisation come to a sudden end?
Most surely it could, through cosmic collision, mismanagement by us and doubtless other causes. But if it does then either we will have established bases elsewhere or other conscious beings have evolved, or will evolve, separately. The completion of the circle, and hence existence, utterly depends on the spread of mentality.

If the aim is to maximise consciousness, shouldn't we be all having dozens of children?
We need to balance the need to create conscious beings with the maximisation of the prospects of their survival and, ideally, fulfilment. We are taking gradual control;

an untrammelled reproductive spree would, under most social circumstances, lead to chaos and misery.

Can there be contact between our present selves and the Alphoma version?

No. Alphoma did exist and will do so again but for the duration of the Nature phase it does not exist.

Where does the theory stand on 'intelligent design'?

It is sacrilege to most scientists to suggest that the process of evolution is anything other than 'random' mutation and survival of the fittest.

Leaving aside the problem concerning the meaning of 'random', many less dogmatic people question whether a hugely intricate entity such as a human being could have come about purely through this objective process.

The suggestion made in this book is that the mutations are in fact controlled to some degree by dark energy. There is still 'survival of the fittest' but there is a force influencing the emergence of new genetic factors.

For this reason it is proposed that there is an element of intelligent design which is created by our Alphoman selves.

If it's true that ideas come from subtly stored data, where does that leave human creativity?

The creative skill comes from the processing of the fragments. The 'nothing from nothing' rule applies in the realm of ideas as well as the material aspect.

Scientists process the raw data looking for combinations which 'fit' and can be expressed as laws. Artists work at a different level – a topic which is briefly explored later.

What if Alphoma is a place of misery?

It can't be because without love and cooperation it could not exist. In any case, Omega will be designed by humans who will, of course, want timeless fulfilment.

The 'transition' following revival sounds suspiciously like the religious idea of purgatory. Is it?

Quite close! It has been suggested that anything which has been believed by very great numbers of people over very long time periods (for example a universal intelligence, a 'fall from grace', a personal resurrection) probably contains a large element of truth. The idea of transition makes sense but, under the interpretation presented here, it will not be punitive.

Why have religions taken such a powerful hold?

They have proved attractive because many of the ideas expressed by religions are, it is suggested, quite close to the truth.

Why is belief in god so pervasive?

It is probably so because our ancestors intuited the role of Alphoma which is a god-like state of omniscience and omnipotence. They also sensed that the development of the universe is subject to an overall guidance. It is a relatively small step to interpret these ideas in terms of an all-powerful protective parent.

There are many other overlaps between religious notions and the account given in this book. For examples; the 'paradise lost' horror of the big bang, the primacy of love, the process of transition to a timeless state of bliss.

Our predecessors saw the universe through a glass darkly whereas we see it with a little more clarity.

Might it therefore be reasonable to say that the theory presented here is essentially a religion?
No gods, no revelations, no churches, no worship, no dogmatism, no deference, no moral judgement of individuals… No.

Why is life so unfair?
There are very many people who live truthful and loving lives who endure terrible calamities; there seems to be no natural justice.

In Nature there is no 'natural justice'. The universe is in transition from almost total turbulence after the Big Bang to complete order. Even allowing for the exponential growth of knowledge and the rapid advances in technological expertise it is almost certainly true that we are at a very early point in the historical process.

There is, therefore, no reason to expect life to be fair. With only the underlying laws and promptings to provide 'shape', nature pursues its evolutionary experiments without regard for individuals. When people speak of 'natural justice' they make the assumption that there is an entity or a process which balances the scales. But there is no such thing.

Thus, an individual caught in an avalanche or felled by a falling tree is not paying for past sins, they just have bad luck. Justice is a proper and necessary invention of self-conscious beings. We should use our growing power to minimise the harm done by the vagaries of Nature but for the foreseeable future we just have to accept that disasters will occur. Nature is not animate, neither is it right or wrong, kind or cruel. The only 'reasons' we need to find for natural phenomena are the forces which determine them.

The case is different, of course, with events which involve human factors. It is legitimate to ask questions about underlying unconscious causes of accidents. But this still does not lead to anything like fairness. The car driver who crashes because of a deep, unrealised impulse towards suicide is not balancing any books for the others caught up in the disaster. They just have the bad luck to be there.

Is there such a thing as 'fate'?
In the river of evolution there is much that is beyond our control. Some have much easier rides than others. But where we are and what happens to us is not individually decided. There is no fate in the sense that our lives are totally determined but of course there are parts of our lives which are completely out of our control and in this limited sense we are 'fated'.

Why are some people more gifted than others?
We are all made up of fragments of Alphoma. Our attributes are determined by the way the bits and pieces fit together. The word 'genius' is perhaps too divisive for comfort but those who stand out as being unusually excellent have better hands of cards than most of us.

What will revival be like?
It will be like wakening after the deepest sleep; it will be as though no time has passed.

What is life in Alphoma like?
All the sweetest dreams are realisable – and we have all the vast historical stuff of the universe to explore!

Is there any point in talking to dead people?
Not if you want an answer! But bear in mind that in Alphoma we'll be able to see all of our lives. It might be fun to be able to show those who have pre-deceased us that we were fly enough to work out what the universe is about.

Probably most of us have done things of which we are ashamed or at least regretful. Will it not be embarrassing to have the details of our lives on display?

In the bliss of Alphoma there will be no painful feelings. We will have total understanding of the psycho-logic behind our actions. There will be no moral judgements and no discomfort.

Why do humans have fleeting feelings of bliss and dread?

Many people have fragmentary tastes of the purest happiness. Many more, sadly, suffer from feelings of deep foreboding.

Both are 'memories'. No individual experienced the explosion of the primal atom but the fact of that disintegration is written into the causal history of the universe. To a small extent we 'know' of the heat, the darkness and the disintegration. The whole truth about the universe is contained within the fragments.

By the same token, we 'know' vaguely about the state of perfect peace. Whenever an individual experiences either of the extremes they are tuning in to small fragments of data about the history of the universe.

The dread which the 'memory' of the explosion generates comes because the historical place and function of that event are not immediately understood. It can be ameliorated by reminding ourselves that although the hellish fires burned they did not hurt any individual and indeed they are a necessary phase of the evolutionary process.

Can there be 'time travel'?

No. Time is abstract; it is the most general expression of the operation of discontinuous energy. We can travel through space and clouds of energy but time has no substance.

For someone from the future to visit us now they

would, of course, have to exist now but they can't, because the future doesn't yet exist. For the same reason, we cannot visit the future.

Neither can we 'travel' to the past. If the past is a place, where is it?

But what about the fact that a clock in a space satellite runs at a different pace from those on Earth?
Clocks, and doubtless other processes, are influenced by the forces operating on them, especially gravity.

But this does not mean that time itself is changed. Earth does not accelerate its rotation nor change its orbital pace around the sun. We can make clocks on the surface of our planet go faster or slower but doing this will not have the slightest impact on our life spans. Just as space cannot be shaped so can time not be warped.

Why do art and music pervade all cultures?
An artist, in whatever medium, generally starts with a blank sheet. Words or shapes or notes are put in some kind of order onto the recording medium. Throughout the process of producing a work of art, hundreds, maybe thousands of decisions are made. The finished work is a summary of all these decisions. However unrelated to the real world it seems, it at least conveys something about the workings of a human mind.

In making the decisions, a line here, a blob of colour there, the artist is delving into the huge treasure chest of the unconscious. The promptings which come to the artist are of a different quality from those seized upon by the scientist. The images are less precise they cannot be formulated into coherent theories, they say nothing that can be tested against reality.

Yet this does not invalidate them. An observer of an art work may not be able to make any significant connection between the shapes and the real world but it is certain that the process of observation causes changes in the observer's brain. There is, in some degree, a process of unconscious communication going on.

The vague notions, expressed by the artist, are to some extent absorbed by the observer, who is changed by the experience. It is quite possible that sometimes the changes are radical enough to produce a shift in physical behaviour but more often than not the new information simply plays its part in shaping future thoughts.

With the words of prose and poetry, the forms produced by dance, the paintings, drawings and sculptures of the artist, there is usually some reference to the real world. Often, referential shapes can emerge without the conscious intention of the artist.

The case with music, the most abstract of the arts, is different. This speaks the most profoundly of ideas and states of being which are only just accessible and which defy linguistic or graphic expression. The composer delves deep into the store. Notions which are too subtle for us, at this stage of evolution, to express in other forms emerge as tunes and rhythms.

When we understand much more, and when technology is very much further advanced, we will be able to show how the process of listening to music changes our ways of thinking. Generally the shifts are too subtle for us to log them even subjectively but occasionally, music causes an observable seismic event in the mind. Conditions have to be just right; we, and probably the performers and the audience about us, have to be in a particularly fortuitous state. Then it can happen that listeners believe that they have gained an inexpressible insight into the most profound and positive depths.

Those who have tried to pin down such relatively rare experiences have sometimes written of 'the timeless moment'. This is, of course a contradiction but it suggests that music can occasionally provide us with the briefest, faintest illumination on the timeless glory that is to come.

Why do many people value art 'originals' so highly?

On a purely objective view it might seem that precise copies would have as much potency as the source work but according to the view offered here, the energy involved in the media is subtly changed by the artists' manipulation. Thus, significantly more information might be picked up from an original than from a copy.

Why do humans love solving puzzles?

This is a sideline, but an interesting one.

In virtually all cultures there are puzzles or ritual reshapings. The almost ubiquitous Cat's Cradle starts with the simple and becomes ever more complex until, in some versions, it reverts to the original. This is a perfect representation of the universal process. Jig saw puzzles also exert a wide fascination and these can readily be seen as simple models of the process of destruction and creation. They show, too, in an approximate way, the necessity of the destructive phase because, obviously, without this there is no challenge and no satisfying process.

People sense that we are all part of a massive 'pass-time' process and the puzzles reassure us that order can and will one day be restored.

How are 'ordinary people' drawn into mass suicide cults?

This is another sideline but one that is also indicative.

Cult leaders usually make absurd claims. Detached observers wonder how anybody could be taken in, yet hitherto sensible citizens abandon their normal habitats and eventually give up their lives.

The account offered here is that those who are vulnerable to cult influences doubtless have a strong sense that death is the quick route to peace. They are not quite as irrational as they often seem.

This might suggest that all of us should therefore take the short cut but although there are times when suicide is an honourable option, the desire for instant paradise is not, on its own, sufficient justification for self immolation.

Is there such a thing as the religious idea of grace?

Probably not as a manifestation of measurable energy but as with words such as 'soul' and 'spirit' the term is linguistically useful, especially in poetry.

Is there any point in prayer?

There being no divine patron in the sky, the ether nor anywhere else, there is no flow of godly energy to humans. However, this does not negate the notion of prayer which has been extant for thousands of years and is therefore likely to have some basis in fact.

The probability, as suggested earlier, is that humans possess considerable powers which rely on relatively weak energy effects. For the time being these forces are beyond the scope of our research instruments but the prediction is that one day they and will be measurable. Evidence for this comes from innumerable personal experiences and from powerful, undeniable phenomena such as the emotion-enhancing effects of crowds which anyone who has attended a football match with thousands of others will know well.

It is by no means unreasonable, therefore, to assume that by focusing the mind some effect on others can be achieved. It is also acceptable to assume that gathering together and focusing multiplies the effect. And research will very likely eventually show that a belief amongst participants that something positive is happening enhances the effect whilst scepticism probably inhibits it.

The outcome is that it is entirely rational to engage in something akin to prayer and to believe that something positive might ensue. But the power of prayer, if it does indeed turn out to exist, is a human one.

By the same token, there is nothing illogical in people gathering, if they so choose, to create the likely multiplying effect which closeness has on the subtler human forces. They will not be asking any other entity for support, they will be making use of their own powers. Research programmes will probably eventually show that such a gathering can produce measurable changes in the brain of a selected recipient. Of course this is nothing new; there are belief systems such as Quakerism which work on the power of collective thought.

It follows from the above discussion that all of the religious efforts over the centuries have not by any means been wasted. The fact that prayer is usually based on belief in a god will surely not reduce its efficacy. However, one big advantage of non-deistic prayer is that it removes the anomaly of asking 'god' to make good something which, if theism is true, the god could have prevented. The earthquake or brutal act which brings about the need for assistance is one of those unfortunate happenings, a consequence of the turbulence caused by the Big Bang. Theists always have the problem of reconciling the idea of a benevolent, omnipotent creator with the suffering of innocents.

Is meditation worthwhile?
Quite often, though by no means invariably, meditation

is associated with getting in touch with some mysterious other plane or an unspecifiable 'other dimension'.

Such constructs are unnecessary. Meditation is surely a very worthwhile activity but it is a form of inner exploration and a way of 'listening' to the subtle 'broadcasts' of other humans and to the background noise of nature.

It is different from ordinary thinking, which involves firing up the conscious aspect of the brain to the highest levels. In meditation, the aim is to switch off as much as possible of the intellectual self-directed babble and to allow the more subtle influences of the unconscious and possibly outside stimulation to register.

Many people who have wrestled with complex problems, or even something as mundane as a crossword clue, have had the experience of putting the struggle aside and maybe going for a walk. The unconscious carries on working whilst we admire the view or listen to the birds and lo! the solution to the problem pops into the conscious mind.

Switching off is sometimes productive and it is certainly a worthwhile thing to do

Is there any point in ritual?

Most who have attended 'rites of passage' will be aware of their potency. Weddings can generate huge quantities of love and joy. Funerals are a very important part of the management of grief.

The abandonment of the notion of a god by no

means entails the loss of ritual. The power of such gatherings comes entirely from the uniting of the subtle human powers. People can devise their own forms of ceremonies for making commitments, welcoming a new child, saying a temporary goodbye to someone who has died and so forth.

There is also no reason whatsoever for non-theists to shun religious buildings. If it is true, as claimed, that our surroundings are subtly changed by events then churches are in general sure to have benign atmospheres for life's rituals.

18 ∘ Worth

*I*n Chapter Three, some tests of the worth of metaphysical theories were proposed. Here is a brief assessment of the theory according to these standards.

1 Coherence
Surely the most taxing notion is that the universe has to be seen as process and structure. This may seem incoherent but, as argued, it is difficult to see how any other formulation can work.

2 Simplicity
Some of the ideas are quite radical and therefore challenging but is hoped that the Digest will help to make things clearer.

3 Logicality
The Digest is structured as a 'ladder of logic'. It seems to work.

4 Science
Reservations about a dogmatic attachment to science have been expressed but generally the theory very strongly supports science and seems not to be contradicted by it.

5 Explanations
The theory offers resolutions to many difficulties including:

- the origin of the universe

- the purpose of our existence

- the impossibility of infinity

- entropy

- how there is life after death

- how determinism and libertarianism can be reconciled

- why and how there are laws of nature

- the relationship between the mental and the physical

- the role and origin of design in the universal process

- where ideas come from

- morality and the roles of love and truth

- why life is so unfair

- thought transference / ESP

- why religion took such a hold

- why humans have fleeting feelings of bliss and dread

- why art and music pervade all cultures

- why humans love solving puzzles

- how 'ordinary people' can be drawn into mass suicide cults

- apparitions

- poltergeists

- near death experiences

- the soul / the spirit

- grace / prayer

- meditation

- ritual

- faith healing

- veneration for old things

6   Predictions

Some predictions generated by the theory are:

- Dark energy will turn out to be the basis for the laws of nature and for 'nudges' which guarantee that Omega will be attained

- Brains engaging in willed activity will show a net gain of (probably dark) energy

- Some brain events will seem, from the scientific point of view, to occur 'at random'. These will turn out to be associated with the exercise of free will.

- We will discover that energy is changed slightly but positively whenever it is subjected to creative activity.

- Subtle forces will be discovered emanating from the brains of conscious beings and these will be found to be capable of acting over long distances and capable of having an effect on physical objects.

o Such subtle forces will turn out to be enhanced by belief in them and by humans gathering with a common purpose.

o There will, most probably, be other self-conscious beings in the universe who will, in the essentials of thought, be like us.

o Ways will be found to deal with vast distances and times.

For related material see
www.universetheory.com

Digest

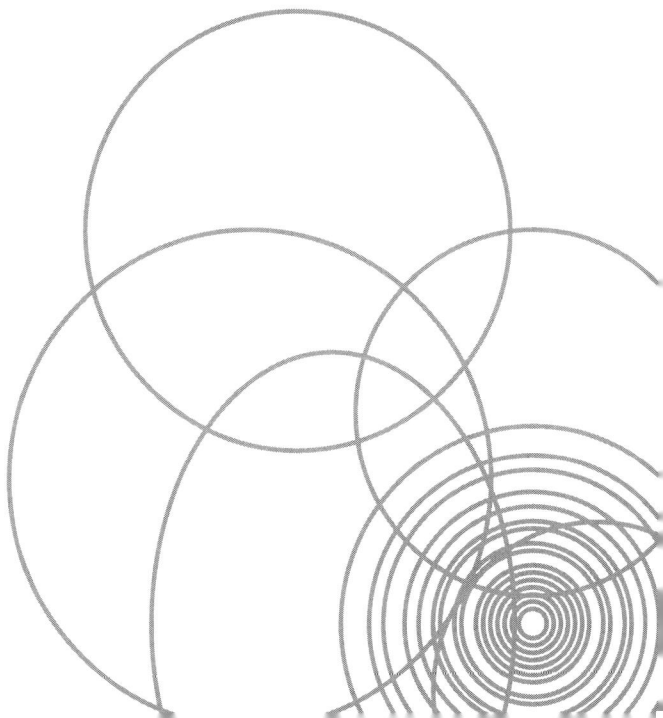

1   This is a theory of the universe. There are plenty already. Why another one?

2   Existing theories are mostly based on revelation or science. Both approaches have great problems which can be avoided by using a metaphysical method as adopted here.

3   'Metaphysics' is taken to mean 'beyond physics'. A metaphysical theory combines proven data with rational speculation. It cannot provide absolute truth; it aims to produce the most satisfactory theory available at the current state of knowledge.

4   There are criteria for judging the merits of any theory including; coherence, simplicity, logicality, compatibility with science, range of explained phenomena, plausibility of predictions.

5   The theory offered here begins with a definition: The universe is taken to be everything that exists, has existed and will exist.

6   It follows that other than the universe there is nothing.

7   'Nothing' is not darkness nor 'empty space'; it is an 'off' command to the imagination. It is literally 'no thing' and is thus unthinkable.

8   The first problem addressed is; how did the universe come into being?

9   Aristotle was surely stating the obvious when he said; nothing can come from nothing. Many other philosophers have agreed. It is conceptually unavoidable that existence has to be taken for granted. Nonetheless this theory provides, amongst many other things, some relief from the nagging ache to understand the nature of existence.

10   Given the vast complexity of the 'taken for granted' universe, forming a theory might seem to be an impossible task. Things clearly have to be simplified and the first move in this process is to assert that, apart from space, everything that exists and happens does so through the operation of energy.

11   'Energy' is not made of anything, it is an abstract notion; energy just is. It can be defined as the essence of everything.

12   The second simplification is to declare that energy operates in space. Like energy, space is not made of anything; it is also an abstraction. However, it is not 'nothing'. It can be defined as the absence of everything.

13   Given that 'nothing' is unimaginable it is reasonable to assume that there is no space without energy and no energy without space. This hypothesis is supported by recent experiments in particle physics which seem to prove that the universe is pervaded by something called 'dark energy'.

14   Taken together the two basic abstractions suggest that the simplest description of the universe is that it is a system of energy operating in space.

15   Emerging from these two fundamentals is time. This comes about because energy presents itself in two forms; the continuous (wave) and the discontinuous (particle). It is the latter which generates time. Like the other two fundamentals, time is not made of anything and is thus also an abstraction. It can be defined as the most general expression of the operation of discontinuous energy in space.

16   As already noted, the task of this theory is to describe, in the most general terms, the operation of energy in space but first it is necessary to dispense with the commonplace but potentially damning notion that the universe is 'infinite'.

17   'Infinity' is here taken to mean 'without limit'. It is, by definition, not imaginable. Anything that can be contained either mentally or physically is self-evidently not 'infinite'.

18   Further, it is impossible to 'prove' infinity by experiment. A super-fast probe might run and run but we could never be sure that it was not just about to hit some cosmic buffers or, more likely, come back like a boomerang. 'Indefiniteness' *is* imaginable and a familiar part of our experience but 'infinity' is unreal.

19   Because 'infinity' is unreal, the universe must be contained. Put in the jargon of philosophers, the sentence 'The universe is infinite' is 'un-cashable'.

20   The finiteness of the universe prompts the question as to what's 'outside' it. The answer can be only 'Nothing'; that is, there is no outside. This means that we are irrevocably within.

21   This leads to a further question; what stops us 'getting out'?

22   Some suggest that space is curved but this will not do. Obviously, gravity causes objects to follow curved trajectories but this does not imply that the underlying space itself is curved. It cannot be so because it is not made of anything. Furthermore, measurements of temperature in space provide strong empirical evidence against inherent curvature.

23   We have only two fundamentals; energy and space. If space is not the containing agent the 'shaping' must be effected by energy. But how can energy provide the container?

24   Modern science has revealed that there are two types of energy, the 'light' and the 'dark'. Dark energy cannot be directly perceived yet it makes up about 70% of the substance of the universe.

25   Scientists have also discovered that the tiny packages and particles (quanta) that make up perceivable energy have extraordinary capabilities. Sometimes they behave as if they are hard and concentrated, at others they behave like waves. Other examples are that they seem to be able to communicate over vast distances and to move

instantaneously from one location to another. And also, against the basic scientific principle that everything is caused, they can seemingly move 'at random'. These phenomena are known as quantum properties.

26 It is here suggested that dark energy, either on its own or aided by quantum properties, sets the limits of the universe such that any long distant probe going 'straight' would eventually return to its starting point. (This might seem very odd but some cosmologists maintain that the universe is organised in such a way that that everything seems to be in the middle).

27 So, the picture of the universe here presented is of a vast ball of energy from which there is no escape. Since it is logically impossible that the universe starts and ends with nothing it is vitally clear that any viable account of the history of energy must be circular.

28 But this throws up a tricky problem in that we know that the universal ball is relentlessly cooling down. In a process called entropy the availability of energy is gradually reducing. If a circular account is to be produced, the running down of energy must somehow be reversed. How can this be?

29 The answer proposed here begins with the observation that living beings experience an inner world of mental events and an outer physical world. Normally we assume that only animals

and humans have these two perspectives but here it is claimed that all energy has subjective and objective aspects.

30   Some entities, animals for example, have a very evident mental life whereas a rock appears to have none. The hypothesis is that inanimate objects do have a mental aspect but it is usually too small for us to perceive. Obviously the seemingly inanimate entities cannot initiate action but is proposed that their energy has an effect on their immediate environments.

31   If it is true that consciousness is a matter of degree rather than some evolutionary 'step' function, what factors govern the balance between the mental and physical elements for any given entity?

32   The proposed answer is that there are two factors which determine the level of consciousness; complexity and dynamism. A rock is a relatively simple object with no moving parts (other, of course, than its constituent atomic particles). A human being is very complex and has many active organs and is thus much more conscious than a rock. But what has this to do with entropy?

33   It is crucially relevant because highly complex and dynamic beings possess will-power. We know of will power at first hand (*a priori* as the philosophers say); it is discernable scientifically only by its effects.

34   It is here predicted that, as the universe evolves,

complexity and dynamism will increase. The entropic decline in the physical aspect of energy will be countered by a growth in the mental aspect. We humans are generators. Doubtless we are still at a relatively primitive stage of the development of the universe but our successors will ensure that will-power steadily grows.

35   For complexity to increase, things have to be brought together. The prediction is that the current expansion of the universe will be gradually reversed through the agency of conscious beings.

36   Eventually the universe will reach a very highly organised state where the physical aspect of energy is at a minimum and the mental aspect at a maximum. This phase can be called Omega.

37   It was noted earlier that any viable theory of existence has to be circular. It follows that this predicted state of maximum consciousness (Omega) must have previously existed. Happily for this theory, science strongly suggests that it did.

38   It is generally held by scientists that billions of years ago all of the energy in the universe was concentrated in an entity which is often called the primal atom. In this theory, this phase is called Alpha.

39   For complete circularity it is essential that Alpha and Omega are absolutely identical. They can thus share a name, Alphoma.

40   It seems almost scientifically certain that something over fourteen billion years ago Alphoma exploded, reducing the wondrous organisation to fragments, converting mental energy to physical and thereby initiating the phase in which we are now living which is called Nature.

41   It is suggested that, aided by the potent universal force of gravity, the purpose of Nature is to re-integrate energy. The universal circle is thus: Alphoma – explosion – Nature – reintegration – Alphoma.

42   It is crucial at this stage to supplement linear thinking (which has been and still is so vital to survival) with what might be called 'structural thinking' which, it is suggested, is utterly essential for understanding. There is time within the circle but overall it is time-free so the universe is both process and structure.

43   For those who are inclined to reject the structural approach it might be useful to reiterate that, because nothing can come from nothing and infinity is unrealisable, a linear account is logically impossible.

44   For Nature to succeed in reintegration, Alphoma must be bonded by a powerful mental force akin to gravity which will eliminate conflict and create a state of maximum desirability. This force can be only love.

45   This powerfully implies that Alphoma is a place

of bliss. If this is so, why does such a beautiful entity explode?

46   It does so because the Nature phase is necessary for the generation of entities with the capability of producing will-power without which the availability of energy could not be renewed.

47   Our successors thus design the universe such that there is freedom in Nature but yet also control which guarantees that the cycle is successfully concluded. (Thus, both determinism and libertarianism are true).

48   It is here proposed that dark energy is the enduring agent of control which operates at two levels, namely the maintenance of immutable forces such as gravity and the delivery of 'nudges'.

49   These 'nudges' are perhaps most evident in the crucial process of evolution which, in conventional scientific theory, depends upon 'random' mutations. Einstein held that every action in the universe has a cause and he was surely right. To a scientist, the word 'random' can mean only 'cause yet to be identified'.

50   The only truly random events come about through conscious acts of deliberately spontaneous thought but the suggestion is that dark energy does not operate at a conscious level but rather provides a machine-like input. It is not a deity, it does not wreak punishments nor bestow favours; its major role is to ensure that Nature stays on track.

51   For there to be choices with real import there have to be 'opposites'; creation/destruction, happiness/sadness and so forth hence, alas, the presence of pain and misery in Nature.

52   These opposites give meaning to the processes of Nature which is like a river contained by totally secure banks. We individuals are tiny fleeting droplets with only partial control over our movements but we all contribute to the flow.

53   A pair of speculative proposals about the 'guidance' of Nature concern information. At the big bang all is distributed but it is suggested that each of the fragments holds bits of information. When we 'rack our brains' we are perhaps trying to fit pieces together. So, when Plato claimed that all learning is remembering he was not far from the truth.

54   The second proposal about information is that every time energy is reorganised it is permanently changed. There is as yet little evidence in support of this but it seems likely and helps to explain a great deal. Perhaps this possible process is facilitated by dark energy.

55   It has been argued that Nature is necessary for the emergence of free will but we all die. What is the point for us?

56   The point is that as Omega approaches, our successors will engineer the revival of every aspect of consciousness, including us of course.

57 They will be able to do this because they will have total control over energy. They will also have a complete map of history because all events, including those caused by acts of will, have causal consequences.

58 They will want revival firstly because of the need to generate power, secondly because the reintegrated universe has to include everything and finally because they will be maximally motivated by love and will want all who have been through the process to share in the blissful rewards.

59 When we die our consciousness ceases to exist. We therefore have no sense of time. At revival time we will be 'instantly' aware of renewed existence.

60 In Alphoma all is love. Clearly most of us have imperfections in this respect. We have to be revived 'as we were' because if change is imposed we would not be ourselves. There must therefore be a process of change which will in no way be punitive and which, given the lure of bliss, will doubtless be almost instantaneous.

61 When all is ready the 'folding in' of Alphoma will take place. Our Alphoman selves will 'exist again' and since there is no individual sense of time for we Alphomans between the big bang and reintegration our lives in Alphoma seem to be continuous.

62 Nonetheless there will be a small temporal element within Alphoma which triggered / will trigger the explosion.

63   The theory produces two moral values, truth and love which are the essentials the success of the universal process. The general precept is that we should aim to lead truthful and loving lives. Where love and truth seem to clash the primary value must be love.

64   The theory also offers some speculative explanations of 'supernatural' phenomena.

65   Finally it is argued that the theory is worthy of consideration because it is logical, coherent and compatible with science and also because it explains many phenomena and makes feasible predictions.

·

For The Young

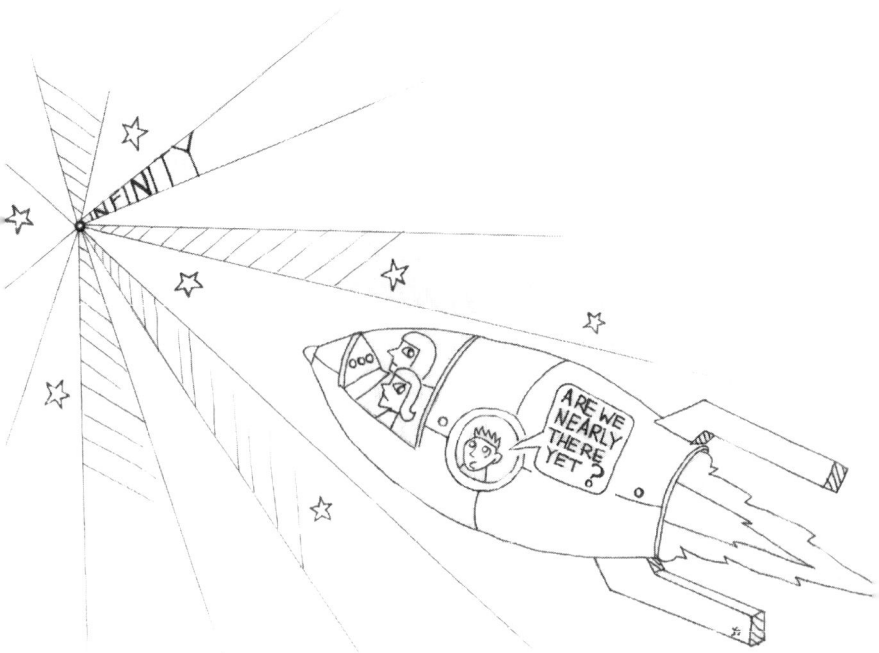

o P   Mummy?

o M   Umm?

o P   Do we believe in god?

o M   No darling.

o P   Gemma says if we don't do what the Catholic god says we'll go to hell when we die.

o M   Aha.

o P   And people with other gods say the same, so we'll have to go to hell again.

o M   I don't think you can go to hell twice my angel.

o P   Maybe we can! Maybe if we don't believe in anything we do a tour of lots of different hells.

o M   Mmmm. What do you think hell would be like?

o P   Not being able to find you… and daddy.

o M   Darling, we'd always find you!

o P   Promise?

o M   Promise!

o P   Cuddle.

o M   Cuddle…

o P   Mummy.

o M   Yes?

o P   What do you believe in?

o M   Mm, that's quite a long story.

o P   Tell it to me.

o M   Well, I'll try. Are you sitting comfortably?

o P   Mummee!

o M   OK. Once upon a time.

o P   Mummeeeeee!

o M   No, I mean it. Most stories have a beginning, a middle and an end but this story goes round

in a circle so I can choose to start whenever
I want.

- P   A circular story?
- M   Yes
- P   And you're going to start a very, very, very long
  time ago.
- M   Clever girl! How did you guess?
- P   I'm a genius!
- M   Then I'd better be careful what I say.
- P   Yes you had! How long ago?
- M   Aproximately fifteen billion years give or take
  a few.
- P   Mummeee!
- M   No, really! Scientists can prove that
  approximately fifteen billion years ago all the
  energy in the universe was gathered together
  in one place.
- P   What's the universe?
- M   It's everything that has ever been, is now and
  ever shall be.
- P   Everything?
- M   Yes, absolutely everything.
- P   Um. And what's energy?
- M   You should ask! All that rushing around in
  the park with Gemma and then swinging
  for forty minutes on the bar. Energy, my
  darling, energy!
- P   But you said that fifteen million…
- M   Billion.
- P   Sorry, fifteen billion years ago all the energy
  was gathered in one place. My park and bar

energy wasn't there – I'd've remembered.

o M   Well in a kind of way it was. Scientists can show that everything in the universe is made of energy.

o P   What does that mean?

o M   Well, this sofa seems solid and simple but if we had a very powerful microscope we'd be able to see that really it's made of tiny packages of energy arranged in a particular way.

o P   Are you kidding?

o M   No

o P   Everything's made of energy, giraffes and the moon, and even Bunny?

o M   Yes.

o P   And even us?

o M   Yes

o P   Oh!… But where does energy come from?

o M   It doesn't come from anywhere and it doesn't go anywhere, it just changes. For example, if we light a log fire it gives out heat, which is a form of energy, and makes smoke and ash, also forms of energy.

o P   Mmm. Curious!

o M   It gets curiouser and curiouser.

o P   So, all that time ago all the energy was bundled together?

o M   Yes my poppet.

o P   What was outside it?

o M   Nothing.

o P   Nothing? Just darkness?

o M   No, not even darkness. Nothing.

○ P   I can't imagine that.

○ M   You don't need to. 'Nothing' is the word that tells you to switch the imagination off. There was all the energy gathered together and that's all.

○ P   No outside?

○ M   Zilch! You don't need to try to think about it.

○ P   I'll try not to.

○ M   That's my girl!

○ P   Mummy!

○ M   Sorry!

○ P   Mmm. But Mummy what did all the gathered together energy make? Maybe an awesome elephant?

○ M   It might have but along with some other people I believe that it was a place of total happiness for billions and billions of people living there.

○ P   Paradise?

○ M   Yes. Paradise.

○ P   It must have been very, very crowded!

○ M   Well no. The people there didn't have physical bodies like we do, they lived in what we call a virtual state.

○ P   I don't understand.

○ M   Well, you know when you're imagining something or dreaming, you know it's not physically real, it all happens in your head?

○ P   Oh! so they were like dreaming?

○ M   Sort of but they had complete control. They could do anything they wanted and make it seem totally real.

- P   So they could have treats all the time?
- M   Non-stop treats.
- P   Yummy! Is paradise still there?
- M   No.
- P   Aww! Why not? What happened?
- M   It exploded, the biggest bang ever!
- P   Oh no! The poor people!
- M   Don't cry my darling; this is a happy story.
- P   How can it be? Such a terrible accident!
- M   It wasn't an accident.
- P   Oh! So it was blown up by bad people? Terribly, terribly bad people?
- M   No darling. Very, very good people.
- P   Good people? How? They blew up paradise? Why?
- M   Remember this is a circular story.
- P   What's that got to do with it?
- M   Well the people of paradise knew absolutely everything and so they knew that for the circle to exist there has to be a time when people are born.
- P   Why?
- M   Because the people who come into being during that time are the ones who live in paradise.
- P   Including us?
- M   Yes.
- P   Yayyyyy!
- M   So through the explosion they created what we call Nature and that's the circle.

○ P   What is?

○ M   Well, there's paradise, then the big bang which shatters the universe into tiny pieces, then Nature which we're living in now and then the bringing of everything back together again so that there's paradise once more.

○ P   But Mummy, after the big bang everything must have been crazy. How did the paradise people know that it would all come together again?

○ M   Clever girl! Things were mad but the paradise people had built in some rules which made energy behave itself. We call the rules 'the laws of nature'. Energy was free but only within certain limits.

○ P   But where were the people?

○ M   There were none. There was only fizzing energy but Nature took its course, with energy following the laws, and billions of years later humans emerged just as the paradise people had planned.

○ P   And, now that we've arrived, it's our job to put everything back together again like a massive jig-saw?

○ M   Yes. Exactly. We are conscious beings with willpower; we are, bit by bit, taking charge of energy.

○ P   But Miss Moverly said that our planet is very, very little, she showed us a map. How could we put everything back together?

○ M   Almost certainly it's not just us, darling. There

are bound to be billions of others on planets
like ours. As time goes by we will make contact
and we'll learn to work together.

○ P   Exciting! But might there be wars like Oliver
in my class says?

○ M   Well, there might but eventually it will be
realised by everybody that to re-create paradise
we need to do two things.

○ P   What things Mummy?

○ M   Most importantly, we need to treat all beings
with love because it's love which will draw us
all together.

○ P   But Mummy, Oliver says that on other planets
there are probably very cunning evil creatures
with sixteen eyes each and worms wriggling
out of their ears and noses and massive teeth
that crunch up babies. How could we
love them?

○ M   If there are such beings we won't have to
cuddle them. If they are intelligent they will
eventually realise that violence is not the way
to regain paradise. But the laws of nature will
have worked throughout and almost certainly
people on other planets will be mostly like us.

○ P   Good. Can we have tea now?

○ M   Can I finish my story first? It won't take
very long.

○ P   OK Mum.

○ M   Thank you. Can you guess what the other
important thing is after love?

○ P   Umm – brushing our teeth?

- M   Nooooo.
- P   Ummmm.... feeding the goldfish?
- M   Not quite. It's truth.
- P   Oooooo – truth!
- M   Yes. It's only by finding the truth of everything that we'll be able to re-build paradise.
- P   Mummy, is that why you're a scientist?
- M   Partly, yes.
- P   Oh.
- M   So what are the two most important things?
- P   Um. I've forgotten.
- M   Poppy!
- P   Errrrrrrrrrrrr. Love.
- M   And?
- P   Errrrrrrrrrrrrrrrrrrrrrrrrrrrrrrrrr. Toothpaste.
- M   Poppy! No treats.
- P   Truth, truth, truth!
- M   Good girl.
- P   But mummy, I've been thinking.
- M   Delighted to hear it.
- P   OK. It's so, so long ago that everything exploded. How will people know how to make paradise again?
- M   Remember, everything is energy and all energy is connected. Every time energy changes it makes its mark, Millions or even billions of years from now the people who come after us will be able to trace a complete map. They'll use the map to bring everyone back to life.
- P   But mummy it'll be such a long time to wait!
- M   There will be a very long time but we won't

know it because when we're dead there's no experience. It'll literally seem like no time at all. We die and the next thing we know we're back in paradise.

o P　　But mummy, what about bad people? They can't be in paradise it wouldn't be fair.

o M　　Most of us do bad things in our lives. The important thing is for us to be living truthful and loving lives at the time we die, then we'll be ready for paradise no matter what we've done.

o P　　But will the ones who aren't loving go to hell mummy?

o M　　There is no hell in the before-and-after life. People who have not become loving and truthful will be given the chance to change which they will surely take because the lure of paradise will be irresistible.

o P　　What's lure?

o M　　Attraction.

o P　　Oh! But Gemma says that bad people have to be punished in terrible fires for all eternity.

o M　　That's such a horrid idea. By the time we are ready to re-create paradise the barbarous idea of punishment will have long ago gone.

o P　　Mummy.

o M　　Yes.

o P　　What have barbers got to do with anything?

Sallorna

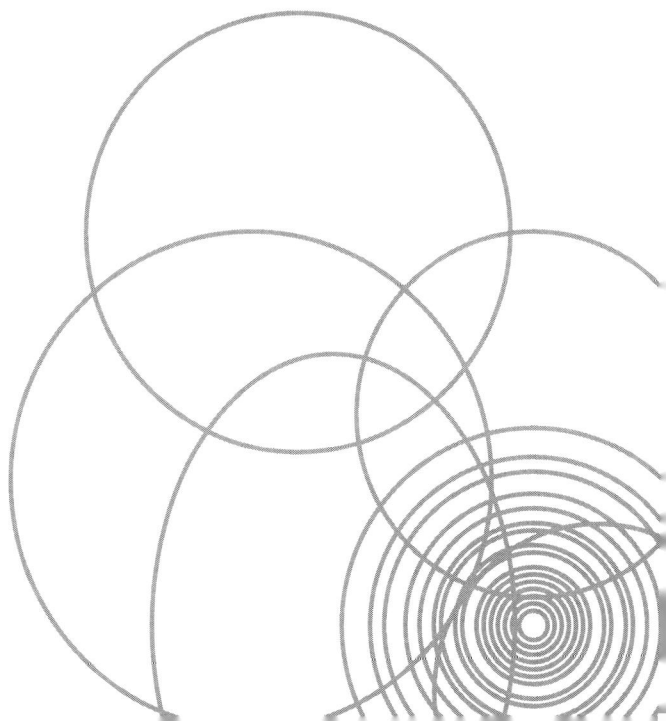

*S*allorna woke. Instantly alert, she glanced at the chronometer above her head and smiled. Unless the instrument were wrong, she had been unconscious for thousands of Earth years. It seemed only a moment since she had started on the journey yet it was not so. She was light-years from home and the mission was apparently on track.

She turned off the capsule life support system and lay, waiting for her body to reach full acclimatisation to the craft's freshly generated atmosphere. 'Hello' she said softly to the picture fixed above her head. It was the one personal reminder in the spacecraft of her past. It showed close family laughing with Ralph, her lover. Her eyes misted slightly but only for a moment. The loss, she firmly believed, was temporary.

Knowing it would be foolish to move too soon, she waited according to the protocol. She desperately wanted to know if her craft had reached the pre-set destination. She also longed to check if the predictions about the development of cosmic object X325BN7687/ Y482TX6358/ Z742SP3440 were anywhere near accurate. Would there be human life and, if so, would it be at a level of evolution where she could have a useful impact? Too little development, or indeed too much, could make her journey futile. But it would be foolish in the extreme to jeopardise the mission through hastiness. What were a few moments in the time span of her journey?

As she lingered, another nagging anxiety pushed into her consciousness. It was altogether possible, likely even, that technology on her own planet had advanced during her absence to the point where problems associated with very rapid travel had been overcome. It could be that when she opened the interior covers she would be treated to the sight of orbiting capsules, with perhaps one of them bonded to hers, awaiting the moment of her awakening.

This she did not want. Yes, in some ways it would be comforting to meet members of the Alliance and to hear what had been happening for the millennia of her coma but she had set her heart on this being her planet and on repaying the total trust granted by her colleagues.

She had almost drifted into natural sleep when the soft gong-like beat came to tell her that it would be safe to move. As she stretched each limb there was no discomfort, only a pleasant awakening stiffness. 'Mmmmm!' she murmured as she lifted her head from the pillow, 'the best sleep I ever had.'

She laughed and swung her legs out of the complex capsule which had held her for the ages of her unconsciousness. Standing was easy. Walking to the covered porthole was no different from the first steps of any day in her Earth apartment. A green light flashing every second told her that it was safe to raise the porthole shield. For the first time in the mission she felt fear, not for her own safety but of failure.

'Come on Sallorna!' she muttered, 'the time of truth.'

She pressed the button. Noiselessly the shield slid. A bright, pinkish light flooded the capsule. Sallorna blinked, adjusting quickly, and then peered out. She could not contain the cry.

'My planet!' she exclaimed, noting immediately, with a surge of joy, that there were no accompanying Alliance craft.

Even without optical aids she could see that there were seas and land-masses, cloud cover and patches of clear sky. 'Just like dear Earth,' Sallorna told herself, 'but is there human life?'

With a single keyed command, she activated the scanners which would field data from 'her' planet. Whilst the essential information was being collected and collated, she took in the essential post-coma nutrients and fluid.

The data which the Alliance scientists had used when planning the journey had, of course, been derived from light which had been travelling for thousands of years. The effectively ancient signs had been that all the ingredients for full evolution had been present on the far distant planet but, as everyone knew, this was no guarantee. There were so many potential pitfalls, natural and man-made, which could have wrecked all progress.

Her repast was over by the time the capsule's computer flashed the message that the initial survey was complete. Shaking with a mixture of anxiety and excitement, Sallorna requested a report. The sound of the automated voice was expected but still it shocked her.

'Sallorna, congratulations,' it said, 'the predictions which you and your colleagues made were very accurate. There is human life here, at various stages of development. For your landing I recommend an island quite close to the equator which I have indicated on the on-screen map. It has stable governance, a tradition of research and scholarship and a benign climate.'

'What's the level of development?' Sallorna asked.

'I would say that the society there is roughly equivalent to the one in Europe in the time of Leonardo,' was the swift response.

'Feed me the most relevant data,' Sallorna ordered.

'The humans are of unfamiliar physiology. You might find them repellent.'

'No matter,' Sallorna replied quickly.

'Shall I include the language?'

'Yes.'

'Are you sure?'

'Yes'

Sallorna felt the familiar mild dizziness as a large amount of information was beamed into her brain. She accessed the new material almost at once and was delighted by the language which was rich in nuance. It was also, like many other tongues in the universe, completely devoid of gender. The universal forms devised by the Alliance allowed for this. Words such 'shee', 'heris' and 'herim' had become familiar.

In her newly acquired tongue, the planet was called Gombran and the target island Itraki.

Not without anxiety she conjured up an image of an Itrakian. The computer had been right to warn her. For all that Sallorna had met many human beings who differed considerably from Earthlings she could not suppress a slight shudder.

The hermaphroditic Itrakians were smaller than most humanoids. Their hairless heads were almost perfectly spherical with eyes to the side as well as the front. There was no nose but the centrally located mouth was large, doubtless because, as Sallorna gathered, this was the route by which Gombranian babies came into their world. Ears were just orifices below the side-located eyes. Like Earthly insects, the people had six limbs but they stood upright. Their clothes were complex and colourful, clearly objects of enjoyment as well as protection against the Gombranian elements.

Sallorna learned that for all the differences, Gombranians shared a great deal of body language with Earthlings, including smiles, nods, head shakes and expressive gestures.

The computer was still taking in information. It told Sallorna that it had identified an individual of high standing and great learning. 'Heris name is Terro-arwah,' the machine said. 'Do you want heris details?'

Within seconds Sallorna knew all about her target. Terro-arwah was coming to the end of a long life. There was a distinguished history of achievement in arts and sciences. Shee was an intellectual colossus with a considerable following; the perfect person for the purposes of the mission.

Sallorna instructed the computer to undertake a final detailed analysis of the atmosphere and to prescribe the medication which would adapt her bio-rhythms to the Gombranian conditions.

When the time was right, she removed all of the life-support clothing which had kept her for so long in perfect condition and stepped into the hygiene chamber to rid her body of all potential contaminants. As soon as the all-clear light flashed, she broke open the packaging which contained the tight-fitting, silver, light-shield suit. Even though she knew that the system had provided precisely the correct level of nutrition, she was delighted that the garment fitted.

Dressed for the next stage of her adventure, she entered the descent capsule which was already primed. In the darkness of night the automated vehicle took her noiselessly to the safe spot the computer had identified. The craft rustled through some dense foliage and came to a gentle stop. 'Perfect!' sighed Sallorna.

Excitement kept her awake until dawn when, characteristically, she was able to doze for a while. She was glad, when she woke, that she hadn't induced sleep with a pill. She took in some further nutrition and fluid before opening the upper hatch and climbing into the smallest of her vehicles, the simple person-transporter, which would take her to Terro-arwah.

The Itrakians had a strong tradition of architecture which employed organic shapes to create highly functional but astonishingly beautiful buildings. Though Sallorna had visited, through the wonders of virtual experience, many inhabited planets she never ceased to wonder at the creative variations devised by humans.

The transporter glided over Terro-arwah's magnificent city and located the great thinker's residence without a hitch. Sallorna knew that her unwitting target would be enjoying heris routine morning walk through a colourful garden not unlike ones which flourish in the Earth's tropics.

Taking care to avoid tell-tale branches, Sallorna brought her simple craft to rest between a wall and a thick bush. Calmly she took her first few Gombranian steps, then stopped, waiting until Terro-arwah's predictable path brought herim close. Then, as unthreateningly as she could, Sallorna called out 'kalyeka' the Itrakian formal word of respectful greeting and parting.

The side-eye that she could see swivelled but the head did not move. Terro-arwah stopped walking and calmly demanded to know who was hiding in the bushes. Sallorna could not tell whether her target was afraid or mildly amused at some presumed prank.

'My name is Sallorna,' she said. 'I come from a distant planet to converse with you.'

The large mouth opened, the head swivelled so that the frontal eyes were directed precisely towards the source of the sound.

'A jester that I hear but don't see,' Terro-arwah said guardedly.

'No jester,' Sallorna said. 'I am able to make myself invisible to you but I can appear whenever you are ready.'

The mouth closed and there was a long pause before Terro-arwah said; 'Either this is magic, in which I don't believe, or a trick.'

'Neither trick nor magic, Terro-arwah, but science, just science in which you do believe.'

'You know my name!'

'Yes, and I remind you of mine. I'm Sallorna.'

There were a few more moments of silence during which the Earthling struggled against an inconvenient urge to laugh.

'Well, Sallorna, I'll play your amusing game. Why do

you choose invisibility?'

'Because people on my planet are of considerably different shape to you and you might at first find me, er, repulsive.'

Terro-arwah moved heris head in a way which Sallorna recognised as politely dismissive.

'I have seen and dissected many strange creatures brought up from our oceans and I think of them as interesting, sometimes even beautiful, despite the differences. Surely you realise that if I am to believe in you, which I scarcely can, I must at least see you.'

Sallorna paused before saying; 'It's different. We have much experience of visiting other planets. Aquatic creatures are one thing, weird-looking beings who can talk and think are quite another.'

The small, round head bent forward. 'Try me!' Terro-arwah said with a touch of humour and waited patiently whilst heris extraordinary visitor pondered.

'Just a first glimpse, then,' Sallorna said.

She knew that Terro-arwah carried no weapons and that if shee attempted to make a lunge towards her, unlikely anyway in view of heris age, she could vanish instantly. The risk was small. She de-activated the light shield and was mildly amused to see a Gombranian expression of deep shock. For a moment she thought that Terro-arwah was going to be sick or, worse, have a baby. Instantly she resumed invisibility and waited for a moment before saying; 'On my planet I am considered to be very beautiful.'

Terro-arwah struggled to regain composure. Eventually shee said; 'Ah well, I suppose that we must seem repulsive to you.'

The fact that shee had thought of this touched Sallorna. 'No,' she replied not entirely truthfully, 'but only because we have seen so many different forms. The fear of the unknown soon goes when there is no threat.'

There was a long silence. Terro-arwah looked around, as though to make sure that shee was unobserved by others. At last shee said; 'Unlike most of my contemporaries I don't believe in spooks and spirits and neither do I think that I am now dreaming. Unless this is a fantastic hoax then I am inclined to believe your tale of travel. Though ridiculed by others I have often speculated that the stars might be suns like our one, with planets similar to Gombran. Yet..'

Sallorna decided to let herim ponder further. At length shee said; 'Please show yourself again.'

Sallorna breathed in a lungful of the thin Gombranian air and took a few steps forward. Instead of turning the light-shield completely off, she adjusted it so that her image was slightly softer than before. Terro-arwah was not fooled. 'No,' shee said, 'the full picture.'

Then the two gazed frankly. Terro-arwah's middle limbs moved in what seemed like a gesture of acceptance.

'What is that strange growth on the top of your head?' shee asked. Sallorna laughed for the first time in heris presence and was relieved to observe that Terro-arwah recognised the noise as unthreatening. 'We call it hair,' she replied. 'Originally it had survival value for the people on my planet but now we think of it as decorative.'

Terro-arwah focused on the light reflecting from Sallorna's auburn tresses and seemed also to smile. 'I can see,' shee said, 'that it could be beautiful. But,' shee went on, pointing in a very Earthly fashion with heris upper right limb, 'your mouth is so small; how can children come from that?'

Sallorna emitted another, involuntary, little laugh and said; 'Babies used to come from our bodies in a different way which I will explain later if you want me to but we no longer have children in such a fashion. We create them via beautiful machines.'

'That sounds heartless,' Terro-arwah quickly responded.

'I'm sure it does,' Sallorna countered, 'but it is far from it. We still have families and love is overwhelmingly our primary value.'

Terro-arwah thought for a moment and seemed to assent.

'Any more fundamental values?' shee asked.

'Truth,' replied Sallorna brightly, to apparent approval.

'And the third?'

'There are no other fundamental ones, only derivatives.'

'What of justice?'

'Justice is a combination of truth and love.'

Terro-arwah seemed on the point of arguing but instead took a deep breath and said nothing.

Sallorna, who had planned to judge things by the moment, made an instant decision.

'I have here,' she said, 'a means of moving about which

is made invisible by a light shield. I have also an invisible base craft some distance away in the jungle where I can sleep and refresh myself. I have tucked it into a remote place where some of your island's dangerous animals ensure that no human will bump into it. I'm going back there now,' she added, 'but I'll return tomorrow at the same time.'

Terro-arwah extended an upper limb, as if to protest, then withdrew it. 'Yes,' shee said, 'it has been an unusual experience to say the least. I need to think and convince myself that I still have my reason. But, before you go, two questions.'

Sallorna assented.

'Firstly, how is it that you speak our Itrakian language like a native?'

'We have machines which can codify speech and then feed the information directly into our brains.'

'Impressive!' said Terro-arwah. 'It takes us many years to learn an alien tongue.'

Sallorna felt that a small tactical advantage had been gained. 'And the second question?' she said.

There was a long pause during which the great Gombranian thinker seemed to become ever easier with the image of Sallorna.

'Yes,' shee at last said, 'it is this. Why have you come here?'

Sallorna allowed more time for, even though she had rehearsed the sentence until the words had almost lost sense, she was acutely aware that this was a crucial moment. She said:

'I have been sent by my people, not just those of my

native Earth but those from all the hundreds of planets in our Universe Alliance of Peace and Progress, to seek your help.'

'Our help?' Terro-arwah queried with an unmistakeable hint of scepticism.

'Yes,' Sallorna said softly. 'I'll explain later.'

There was a subtle shift of mood.

'You say you want help but how do I know that you are not here to take over our planet? So often do those who declare for peace have a warlike agenda and you are evidently so clever, so powerful.'

'It is my job to persuade you that I come in peace,' Sallorna said. 'If I cannot convince Gombranians, through you or some other leader, then I will leave.'

'To go back to your planet?' asked Terro-arwah.

'No' said Sallorna, 'to die.'

The sage, seemingly shocked, was ready to formulate another question but Sallorna cut herim off.

'Tomorrow!' she said and instantly vanished from Terro-arwah's view.

○ ○ ◯ ◯ ◯ ○ ○

Terro-arwah was waiting. 'Come,' shee said as soon as Sallorna had revealed herself, 'there is a place in my garden where nobody will disturb us.'

Shee led the way into a shady spot which had comfortable seats.

'What help do you seek?' Terro-arwah asked with a wariness which came close to hostility. Sallorna judged that heris night time thoughts had been more about danger than opportunity. She said; 'I will have to explain a great deal before I can answer satisfactorily.'

'So be it.'

'But ask questions at any point.'

'Rest assured, I will.'

Sallorna then said; 'Firstly I must give you a summary of what we in the Universe Alliance believe about the universe.'

'That would seem to be a useful starting point,' Terro-arwah responded, with a hint of irony. Sallorna knew that for a proud and original thinker it might be invidious to be lectured to by an apparently youthful stranger but there was little choice. She smiled briefly and began.

'Well, let's begin by talking about the size of the universe.'

'Surely, it's infinite. Utterly without limit.'

'So it has been said for most of history but we have an excellent reason to reject the notion because we can accurately measure its extent and mass.'

Terro-arwah made an unambiguous expression of surprise.

'In fact, as we'll discuss in a moment, the size changes but there can be no doubt that it is a contained system.'

'I will have to take your word for it, of course, but I would like to know, if indeed the universe is finite, what your great scientists think lies outside it.'

'Nothing.'

'But surely "nothing" is unimaginable and therefore meaningless.'

'Well, in fact we take the view that it is infinity which is unimaginable. The point about "nothing" is that we don't have to imagine anything. That's its meaning. No thing. It's an instruction to ourselves to stop the process of imagination.'

Terro-arwah's expression of dubiety intensified.

'Well, we might debate these things for some time but supposing, for the sake of argument only, that I accept that the universe is a self-contained thing of a measurable size, what if one day it bumps into another huge finite entity. Would that be two universes or one?'

'Our practice is to use the word "universe" to refer to everything that exists so we would have to change our view of the universe.'

'Not impossible, surely?'

'By no means impossible, but there is a very sound principle of science which says that we should deal only with what we've got. There's no point in pure speculation, other than for the purposes of enjoyable fantasy, because pretty much anything is possible in theory.'

Terro-arwah nodded. 'In fact, we too have such a principle of economy of concepts and it is one I support. And what you are saying is that in this case we have a closed system with no evidence whatsoever of the existence of anything else.'

'Exactly.'

'None?'

'None!'

'Very well,' Terro-arwah said, 'because I am keen for you to go on with your account I will accept the idea that the universe is finite though vast.'

'Thank you, but at the risk of driving you away altogether I now have to reveal that although the universe is now vast, it was once exceedingly small.'

'Oh, come now! How can that be? Even if all the heavenly bodies were piled into a single heap it would surely be a very large heap.'

'It would, but we have discovered that things are not what they seem.'

'Now you are talking of mysteries.'

'Not at all. The proven scientific fact is that everything within the universe is made of something we call energy. This seemingly solid bench on which I am sitting is in fact composed of tiny particles. Some of these particles orbit other ones, just as planets go round the sun. But the particles are not solid. They are all made of energy. It is the universal substance.'

Terro-arwah made a rueful face. 'How interesting. One of our ancient thinkers postulated something along these lines but shee was ridiculed.'

'Often the way, alas,' Sallorna commented. Terro-arwah, in a fashion which Sallorna was beginning to recognise as characteristic, took time before saying;'So I take it that this energy is neither solid, liquid nor gas?'

'Correct. It's elusive, ephemeral. You see manifestations of energy shooting across the sky in an electrical storm, sunlight is energy, heat from your fires is energy. Sometimes it seems almost like a facet of nothing, though we tough-minded scientists tend not to speak in such terms. We have devices which can see into the innermost workings of things and all we see, whatever we investigate, is energy.'

'So you are telling me that when the universe was small there were no solid objects but just a condensed collection of this stuff you call energy?'

'In a way, yes.'

'But I still don't understand. Surely the stock of energy in the universe must remain constant because, if it is finite as you say, there's nowhere for it to go. How can there be less energy in the condensed version?'

Sallorna looked at her companion. By this time she was totally at ease with the physical differences, she could even see that there was a magnificence, a magisterial dignity which, knowing that Terro-arwah was unable to determine the time and manner of heris death, brought her some sadness.

'Well? I await,' Terro-arwah said with a reassuring touch of amusement.

'You are absolutely right,' Sallorna responded, 'The stock of energy does remain constant but now we need to take another step in the exposition.'

She marshalled her thoughts for a moment before saying:

'You are very aware that we humans can experience the physical world around us but that we can also look inwards. We have a physical aspect to our lives but we also have a mental one.'

'With that I have no problem whatsoever, although the relationship between the two is deeply puzzling.'

'Quite,' said Sallorna, smiling. 'But, leaving that complexity aside for the moment, the next stride is to accept that mental activity is dependent on the workings of the brain which, like everything else, relies on the operation of energy,'

'I'll have to take your word for that, but do go on.'

'Well, our theory is that when the universe was physically very small, most of the stock of energy was being used for mental activity.'

'You say 'theory'; why can't your wonderful scientists test this proposition?'

'Because science has no direct access to the workings of mental energy. Science deals with the outer, that is, with what we sometimes call "the real"'

'Surely thoughts and feelings are real?'

'Indeed so, to the individual who experiences them they are real but I'm sure that you are all too aware of the distinction between the subjective and the objective.'

Terro-arwah waved one of heris upper limbs and smiled. 'Of course,' shee said distractedly before lapsing into deep thought. Sallorna waited patiently until her puzzled pupil spoke again.

'So, you are suggesting that this physically condensed version of the universe was in fact a body of thought?'

'Yes, but not entirely so. We hold that there was a small core of physical energy, the universal brain so to speak which was the basis for all the mental activity.'

'This is proven?'

'No. It's also hypothesis but maybe you might be persuaded to accept it when you have heard the remainder of our arguments.'

'Time will tell but first; does this vast mental entity have a name?'

'We call it Alphoma.'

'But it does not exist now, as we speak?'

'No.'

'So, pray, what happened to Alphoma?'

'It exploded.'

'It what?'

'Blew up, like a Gombranian volcano, only much, much more so.'

Terro-arwah's jocular mood disappeared. Shee seemed almost impatient.

'You're going to have to work hard to convince me of this,' shee warned.

'Oh,' said Sallorna, 'the explosion which, rather simplistically, we call the Big Bang is incontrovertible. Science can prove that it happened. The condensed universe cracked open and the stock of energy was instantly converted from the mental form into the physical. All that thought was partially replaced by solidity and heat and brilliant light.'

'Partially?'

'Yes. You'll probably be surprised to hear that easily the majority of the energy in the exploded universe is invisible to humans. I'll tell you more of that later.'

'I'll wait impatiently but in the meantime tell me the name of the exploded phase.'

'We call it "Nature".'

Terro-arwah smiled and said, 'Yes, of course; Nature.'

There was yet another contemplative silence eventually broken by the Gombranian.

'So, presumably after the explosion the universe expanded very rapidly.

'Yes. It's still expanding.'

'Into nothing?'

'Yes. As energy pushed out, space was created.

The two are interdependent. Without energy there is no space.'

'But something must have kept things in some kind of order because one thing we have observed from Gombran is that the movements of the cosmic bodies are very regular.'

'Indeed. There were forces operating right from the start. One of these we call gravity.

It's relatively weak but it managed to pull some things together. It's what keeps your three lovely moons in place.'

Terro-arwah pressed an upper hand to heris cheek for a moment, a gesture which Sallorna found endearing.

'I've often wondered about that,' shee said.

'Gravity is one of the forces which guarantee what we call the Laws of Nature. These forces operate throughout the universe and they are what make science possible. We believe that they are mediated through dark energy.'

Terro-arwah got to heris feet and began to pace slowly, deep in thought. Sallorna remained silent until shee said, 'Alright, please continue.' Sallorna obliged.

'In the first phase after the big explosion, the universe was a fearful place. Mental activity was at a minimum, the physical dominated. There was extreme heat and cold, explosions, crashings, dreadful noises.

'But slowly gravity introduced a modicum of order until millions and millions of years after the explosion, planetary systems such as yours and the one I come from were formed.'

Terro-arwah nodded, as though giving permission for Sallorna to continue.

'Over aeons the planets cooled and on some of them there began a process which we call evolution. The basic laws of nature bring energy together in what seems like a huge series of experiments. Some combinations didn't last but others did. The more complex arrangements of energy also interacted, producing even more sophisticated forms. Through this process, and over a very long period of time, the first signs of life appeared. This took many forms but a very obvious one, here and on many other planets, is vegetation.'

'Once again we have a classical philosopher who suggested such a process. Shee wrote about the survival of the fittest.'

'A thinker ahead of heris time,' Sallorna said. 'That's precisely the process. In the workings of evolution some things survive because they are adapted to their environment. And once life forms emerged, vegetation, aquatic life, animals, the plants and creatures handed down the recipe for survival success. It's a process which is guaranteed to produce winners.'

'Culminating, so far at least, in humans,' Terro-rwah said with evident excitement.

'Indeed,' Sallorna said, 'but with humans came a massive change. Animals have consciousness, of course, and higher forms may have some rudimentary self-consciousness but humans are different. When we came on the scene there was, for the first time since the Big Bang, an identifiable mental aspect to the universe. It was tiny, of course, in relation to the physical immensity but it was something like candles spluttering into life in a vast sea of darkness.'

'Some of the candles have evidently been burning longer in some places than in others,' Terro-arwah offered. It seemed to Sallorna almost like an apology and she smiled. 'True,' she said. 'But it's what Earthlings would describe as the luck of the draw.'

The ensuing short silence was slightly uncomfortable but Sallorna felt that great psychological progress had been made. She was the first to speak.

'Of course, humans changed the nature of evolution radically. We produced language, methods of recording information, theories and, crucially, ways of harnessing power. We have not always used the power wisely but overall the balance has shifted very considerably. In the early times of human evolution, physical forces were dominant. An earthquake, an eruption, drought, pestilence and many other natural phenomena were to be dreaded. Now we can predict, escape or, even better, control; humans are more and more in charge. We have discovered wondrous things about the nature of energy which promise to deliver us not just dominance over Nature but total power.'

Terro-arwah shuddered, a piece of body language which Sallorna instantly understood.

'I see your anxiety,' she said softly.

'Well,' the Gombranian answered, spreading heris four upper limbs wide, 'can this be good? Here we revere Nature, some even worship it. Humans are so fallible, so self-seeking. Absolute power is surely a guarantor of disaster.'

Sallorna reached up to caress the silvery leaf of a nearby bush. The texture was that of satin and the tendrils on the underside seemed to charge her fingers with creative energy.

'The worry is entirely understandable. All of the planets in the Alliance have histories involving examples of terrible abuse of power but this is the nature of the evolutionary process. As will, I trust, become clearer as I tell you more about our beliefs, the struggle is inevitable as is the gradual growth of understanding. However tempting it is to cling onto innocence, all attempts in the history of the universe to stifle the growth of knowledge have eventually failed.'

Terro-arwah nodded. Shee confirmed, with some reluctance it seemed, that this was true of Itrakia which was just emerging from a dark, repressive century.

The leaf which Sallorna was fingering came away from its fixing. She felt embarrassed and begged forgiveness. Terro-arwah laughed and politely dismissed her worries. 'The leaves are harvested and used for the healing of skin,' shee said. 'Those ones are just about ready. Try it; rub the smooth side on your cheek.'

Sallorna complied and immediately felt a blissful warmth which spread deliciously throughout her body.

'See!' said Terro-arwah, with a hint of pride, 'they have power even over a visitor from another planet.'

Heris guest was so engrossed by the sensations that it was a shock when Terro-arwah prompted her.

'So, Sallorna,' shee said, 'what are the members of your mighty alliance going to do when they have acquired total power?'

'Our alliance!' Sallorna said. 'All of us.'

Terro-arwah smiled. 'Well, then, what are we going

to do?' shee conceded.

Sallorna let the leaf fall to the ground and rallied her thoughts.

'We are going to re-create Alphoma,' she said.

Her pupil registered gratifying shock.

'Surely not remotely possible!' shee declared. Sallorna smiled and said;

'We believe it is. We think that it is the ultimate goal of all human endeavour.'

'But how could it be? Engineering on such a vast scale is surely beyond human ingenuity.'

'Not so. As I said, humans, in full cooperation with each other, will gradually acquire total knowledge and complete potency.'

'But why would you, or as you insist, we, want to do that; to re-create something which is destined to self-destruct?'

'Well, we think that the cycle happens only once.'

'So it's both historic and in the future? How can that be?'

Sallorna knew that this would be one of the major stumbling blocks to the success of her mission. She took a little while to compose her thoughts before saying:

'Terro-arwah, you are a scientist. You observe the world around you and you conduct experiments. You formulate hypotheses and you test them. When you think you have established a series of truths you link them into theories.'

'All this is gladly agreed.'

Sallorna nodded and persisted with her theme. 'You have accepted, as billions of other humans have, that the linear way of thinking, which deals with cause and effect, is extremely productive.'

'Indeed so. What else?'

'Well, you have also found, in common with so many others, that the linear approach has its limitations. It breaks down when we try to form a complete theory of the universe because if a 'first cause' is postulated then the notion of universal causation is thereby abandoned. And if we don't postulate a first cause we have to invent the impossible notion of infinity.'

'I'm still not persuaded by your disdain for this concept.'

Sallorna hesitated for a moment, searching for another form of expression but eventually deciding to say;

'All I can do is point out again the logical impossibility of the idea. If infinity is a real thing it cannot, by definition, be imagined because if our imaginations could contain it, it would be finite.'

Terro-arwah showed signs of slight irritation.

'But what's the alternative? Pure moonshine?'

'No. We have to accept the dual nature of the universe. It has two phases or aspects, the physical and the mental. The scientific approach is totally appropriate for the physical aspect of existence but the mental aspect is altogether more subtle. We have to school ourselves to think in a different mode where time assumes a different character. It takes practice but after a while it becomes easier. The two phases are totally interdependent. In one phase, time is manifest, in the other, it is not. And in the phase where there is no time, it makes no sense to think in terms of cause and effect.'

Terro-arwah gestured and Sallorna understood that shee needed time to digest these ideas. At length shee said:

'I will, as you suggest, need to practise this change of thinking but whilst I do so I'd like to tax you with another question which has been troubling me.'

Sallorna smiled once more. 'Please. Ask away.'

Terro-arwah's expression was more of a grimace than a grin.

'You say that Alphoma is a mental state. That presumably means it must have identity.'

'In a manner of speaking, yes.'

'Then who is it? The god in which so many believe?'

'No, not god.'

'Then?'

This was yet another big step for Terro-arwah to take and Sallorna decided to soften her certainty.

'We cannot yet know for sure but we believe very strongly that Alphoma contains all the consciousness generated by the processes of Nature.'

Sallorna thought that if Gombranians could whistle in surprise then this is what Terro-arwah would have done. Instead there was a gasp. Undeterred, Sallorna continued.

'Alphoma houses every single person, every bit of animal consciousness, even that tiny, fragmentary element which attaches to the simplest manifestation of energy.'

'You're saying that objects such as plants have consciousness?'

'To a very, very tiny extent; yes, everything does.'

Terro-arwah pondered. At length shee said;

'The prospect is frightening, especially so since you said earlier that your wonderful science cannot directly investigate Alphoma. You believe that Alphoma contains all consciousness. Is it not possible that Alphoma might be the very pit of terror?'

Sallorna shook her head gravely.

'It's true that we cannot inspect Alphoma as a complete entity,' she said, 'but there is a source of information which makes us very confident indeed that we are on the right track.'

She saw that the Gombranian was waiting attentively so she continued.

'I have absorbed your writings and I know that you have made a special study of the people you call mystics. As you have so clearly recorded, these thinkers come from many ages in your history and from diverse cultures. They eat and drink to the minimum and instead of concerning themselves with the world around them, as most of us do, they focus inwards.'

'Indeed,' Terro-arwah confirmed, 'and I think I see what you are getting at. Without exception the mystics reach the conclusion that blissful unity will be the final state of the universe and that, in that unity, each individual will have god-like powers. But, as I concluded in my book, these ideas can have no great status. Ultimately we have to dismiss mystics as fantasists, dreamers; people literally not of the real world.'

'So it might seem,' Sallorna said, 'but the truth is that on every planet in the Alliance we have the same phenomenon. The explorers of the mental interior almost invariably come up with the same picture.'

Terro-arwah seemed exasperated.

'But, if I may speak thus, so what? They claim to be seeing into the future, not researching the past.'

'It is very understandable that they think so but the truth is that if Alphoma once existed and will exist in identical form again, then the mystics are both reporting and predicting.'

The movement of the four upper limbs spoke volumes of Terro-arwah's agitation.

'But surely you don't think that they have access to the future. How could that be scientific?'

'No, we don't think that.'

'And according to you, Alphoma was a mental state which was not accessible to science but in any case it was smashed to tiny pieces. It is surely doubly unavailable.'

Sallorna could not help raising a hand in what she instantly realised was a teacher-like gesture, one she regretted. Happily, Terro-arwah seemed not to notice.

'I agree that that would seem to be the case but please bear in mind that Alphoma was a very highly organised state. Energy was at its most efficient arrangement. You could imagine it as a beautiful structure or perhaps a three dimensional picture.

'When the explosion came, everything was distributed but we have discovered, improbable though it might seem, that each tiny fragment of energy contains information. These fragments are segments of the great picture. For reasons which I'll explain later, some of this data helped to shape the physical development of the universe but at the moment we are talking about the mystics and their sources of information.

Terro-arwah smiled. 'May I hazard a guess?' shee asked. Sallorna nodded, also smiling and knowing that the great mind was racing.

'You are going to tell me that the human brain is the most complex entity to have emerged, at least thus far, and that it's composed of information-bearing fragments of the Alphoma picture. Mystics just happen to have fortuitous arrangements of energy which make more sense.'

'Precisely! And they work hard mentally to move their particular pieces around, to try things out, to derive some hint as to the overall meaning. It's like peering through a mist or, as one of the early religious leaders on Earth put it, through a glass darkly, but they can see more than we can.'

'But if there's this mystical picture available, surely there must be other information about the physical world which could be derived from this source.'

Sallorna smiled and waved her hands acceptingly.

'There is,' she declared. 'That's where ideas come from.'

Sallorna judged that it was right to allow time for reflection and it was the Gombranian who broke the silence.

'One of our ancients here in Itrakia, a thinker called Zibonda whose thoughts have shaped our intellectual development, put forward the idea that all learning is a kind of remembering.'

Sallorna clapped her hands.

'It never ceases to amaze me. We too had such a one,

a philosopher called Plato.'

'If what you are saying is correct then both our Zibonda and your Plato were right, though I'd prefer to express it that all inspiration is remembering because learning, at least without your miraculous machine, is very often just hard work.'

'I agree absolutely,' Sallorna said, 'but the principle that there is inherited information surely has to be accepted. It's the simplest hypothesis and, as I say, we can show that energy is coded.'

'So this is also perhaps the source of artistic inspiration?' Terro-arwah suggested.

'Surely! Artists also see through a glass darkly. They cannot give us precise pictures but they provide profound sketches of the truth.'

'Especially musicians?'

'Yes!'

'Sing me something from your planet,' Terro-arwah demanded suddenly and totally unexpectedly. Sallorna felt foolishly embarrassed and protested that she had no voice and in any case could not think of anything. The Gombranian refused to accept these excuses. 'Here's one of our Itrakian tunes,' shee announced. 'When you have heard it you will have no choice but to return the favour.'

Though she knew a great deal about the universality of humanity, Sallorna was pleasantly surprised and delighted by Terro-arwah's assumption of polite reciprocity.

There then began a noise which seemed to go direct to Sallorna's heart. There were no words, only a succession of sounds which changed in quality as though members of an Earthly orchestra were playing in sequence. At times it seemed as though Terro-arwah was capable of creating a duet or even a trio from the single mouth. Though she had resolved never to cry whilst on her mission, Sallorna could not stem the first prickling of tears.

'I can't follow that,' she declared when the tour-de-force was over. Terro-arwah countered that she could and must.

There was a long silence. Terro-arwah waited patiently, seemingly confident that shee would get her way. Sallorna sighed. 'Alright,' she said. 'It's the only one where I can remember the words.'

The Gombranian nodded encouragingly and was then treated to a wavering, moderately accurate rendition of the Brahms lullaby.

'Beautiful!' Terro-arwah said when it was over. 'The universal language.'

'My mother taught me that,' Sallorna said, 'but she could really sing.'

'It could not have been more moving,' Terro-arwah replied.

And it seemed then that the force had fled from their exploration of ideas. They agreed to go their separate ways and to meet the following morning.

○ ○ ◯ ◯ ◯ ○ ○

For the first time since her revival from the coma Sallorna felt uneasy. It was not that things were going badly, far from it, it was that, despite the rigorous training, the human aspects of her work were in danger of weakening her resolve. It had all seemed so academic and, at the same time, so carelessly adventurous when the mission was being planned but now she was facing the truth; this was real. Terro-arwah was a fully fledged human being and she was proposing to intervene on a dramatic scale in the development of heris life and indeed, eventually, that of the entire huge planet.

Instead of returning immediately to the capsule she embarked on a transporter tour of the island, skimming silently and invisibly above the cities, towns and villages. The beautiful Itrakia was very primitive by Alliance standards and Sallorna saw many circumstances where she knew that an intervention from her could have spared much suffering. Yet she knew it would be very damaging to her mission if she were to appear suddenly to unsophisticated people.

She saw also many examples of human joy. The open air schools seemed mostly to be happy places, many families worked well together, there were artists everywhere and their work was highly valued.

Sallorna parked her craft on an unpopulated purple beach which was washed by a gentle, emerald green sea. Richly coloured, complex flowers adorned a low cliff which defined the landward boundary of the strand. She strolled for a while, then sat, absorbing the peace. Further doubts trickled in to corrode her certainties. There were so many examples of good outcomes. Alliance statistics proved beyond doubt that intervention was the most humane policy yet there had been not a few counter-examples. 'Supposing Gombran is one such?' Sallorna thought. 'Left to themselves they may develop ideas which even the mighty Alliance would find new and wonderful.'

Deeply troubled, she decided to return to her orbiting spacecraft for the night. There was energy a-plenty thanks to the re-charging power of the Gombranian sun. She docked the shuttle and entered her home. Immediately the picture of her loved ones caught her eye and she fought against tears. She had resolved to be strong. It had been her intention never to use the simulator but the loneliness overwhelmed her.

With tears still flowing, she donned the helmet. She knew that the virtual experience would be less potent than it had been on Earth because no other real person would be connected to the system but in this, of course, she had no choice. Thanks to the fact that her family and friends had all contributed large amounts of personal data, the computer would do a very convincing simulation.

She set the parameters, choosing a rural, hilly, verdant setting close to a blue sea. The weather, she decided, should be summery for a garden party. She specified most of the cast but demanded that all of her real memories of her lover, Ralph, were to be temporarily suppressed. She wanted to meet him afresh. Setting the time at three months before the start of her mission, so that her departure would be a big topic of conversation, Sallorna activated the device and was instantly on Earth.

The wonder of virtuality allowed her to be aware that she was in an unreal world but it provided her with every experience as though real, from the warmth of the sun on her back and the smell of the grass to the light of love in the eyes of her family.

In the scenario she was home from training and all her familiars greeted her warmly. Benign strangers, created by the computer, were introduced. Several of them were interesting and the conversation flowed, some of it flirtatious. Missing interaction with her own kind, Sallorna determined that she would find at least a temporary love.

All the newcomers wanted to know about her courageous plans. Her family and friends reiterated that they didn't want her to go yet almost all said that the trip was right and that they could not imagine anyone better equipped than she to make it a success.

Sallorna felt strength gathering. There was sadness at leaving everyone but abundantly there was confidence that in Alphoma they would all be together. Her mother, perhaps the one with the most to lose, was certain. 'It's your destiny, darling, a great honour. We will content ourselves with the virtual you until we are all reunited,' she declared.

A brother, Graham, something of a rebel, spoke strongly against her coming mission but others put the irresistible arguments and said that Graham took this stance only because he was jealous or could not bear to think that his beloved sister was going away.

When Ralph appeared, a stranger as she had ordered, her heart instantly reacted. The loveliness was multiplied. Everyone loved him, all could sense their rightness for each other. Sallorna spilled some wine on her clothing thus making an excuse to change into a dress which appeared to make Ralph reel. They laughed and touched and shook with the force which flowed between them.

She had specified romance. The computer cooperated. She had requested love and sensuality and she was not let down. In the afterglow, Ralph said that he could not bear to lose her yet part of his love was generated by her determination, her courage, her willingness to postpone delight in the service of the universe. His words were: 'The loss will be temporary. We will have our simulations. You must go.'

The virtual session over, many Earth days compressed into minutes of Gombranian time, Sallorna returned to her reality with a delicious warmth of mind and body, with memories of romance and of bliss. Her doubts were banished. She knew, of course, that the voices and the views had been simulated but they had been entirely true to her Earthly life and she felt once more courageous.

○ ○ ◯ ◯ ◯ ○ ○

The protagonists were in business-like mood as the conversation resumed. Terro-arwah seized the initiative.

'We were talking yesterday of the mystics. Your claim is that they have something very useful to say. They themselves generally believe that they are experiencing the future, or at least something which exists perpetually, but you are saying that their information is coming from the past which, if your reconstruction of Alphoma turns out to be possible, will also be the future.'

'That's what we intend.'

'So, the universe is a three stage process; Alphoma,

Nature, Alphoma?'

'In a way, yes, but we think it's more accurate to see it as in two parts; Alphoma and Nature.'

'But you said that Alphoma preceded the big bang.'

'Yes.'

'And you are also saying that our successors will create Alphoma?

'That too.'

'So in what sense are the two manifestations of Alphoma one and the same?

A powerful memory of the garden party and the ensuing loveliness came to Sallorna and she had to work to push it back into her unconscious so that she could focus on her words. Terro-arwah looked intently at her as she hesitated but seemed to understand that the pause was nothing to do with intellectual uncertainty. Sallorna said:

'They are so, we believe, because they are identical in every way and because, in its mental aspect, Alphoma is timeless. The people of Alphoma existed prior to the Big Bang and they will exist again when it is reconstructed. They are not aware of any gap just as I had no perception of time during my very long journey from Earth.'

This time the silence was of Terro-arwah's choosing. Shee broke it with the observation that timelessness is a difficult notion.

'Indeed' Sallorna replied, 'but again, if I may be so bold, you yourself have written very eloquently about what you have called 'the timeless moment' and about the tricks that dreams and spells of unconsciousness play with our experience of time.'

'Yes, I have had some intimations, especially when listening to music, or enjoying nature or appreciating art, where time seems to be suspended. Timelessness is not an entirely alien concept. But I'm struggling with the physical implications. Surely, whilst energy is operating, time must exist.'

'In the physical domain, yes. Our belief is that in Alphoma there is a residual physical core but this, we suggest, generates a vast seamless envelope of mental activity which has no discontinuity and therefore has no real time.'

'So eternity is banished as well as infinity?'

Sallorna nodded firmly. 'Indeed. It is another word without sense. It's an unrealisable notion and therefore meaningless. One of our early philosophers, a man called Aristotle, said, "How can one conceive of an actually infinite series? Nothing actually infinite can exist.' But despite this wisdom, people on Earth persisted in speaking of infinity and eternity for ages and ages, causing vast disquiet and confusion.'

'But it is not the case that people in Alphoma lose all sense of time?'

'No, they enjoy what we call virtual time which is theirs to control. Virtual time is the servant of consciousness not its tyrant. We have devised machines which create virtual worlds which are so vivid that they seem completely real yet we can control them, set the parameters so to speak.'

Terro-arwah said: 'I think I begin to understand why you sometimes seem to speak of Alphoma as having two existences and sometimes only one but there's another profound barrier blocking my route to understanding.'

Sallorna felt a huge surge of well-being. It was, she thought, one of those rare portentous moments when vital streams converge and merge. She smile radiantly and was rewarded with reciprocal warmth.

'Please. Ask,' Sallorna said.

'It's this,' Terro-arwah began. 'However much you emphasise the unitary nature of Alphoma there's no escaping the fact that this wonderful creation exploded and thus generated the phase you call Nature. If my understanding is correct, you are saying that the overall purpose of Nature is to generate ever more self-conscious beings who acquire more and more power. These beings will, you claim, design and then create Alphoma.'

'Nicely put!'

'Including setting up the parameters, presumably via the laws of nature, which guarantee that the process will work out.'

'Well, not just the laws because a system built entirely on laws would not give us the essential opportunity to develop will power. There has to be freedom but, as you say, there have to be controls which ensure that the re-creation of Alphoma eventually takes place.'

'So?'

'So. There is a universal principle that nothing happens without a cause. Some of the causes are forces of Nature and some are efforts of will. But for many centuries on Earth it was widely held that some things happen at random.'

'Ah, random – a tricky fish.'

'Tricky indeed, particularly for a scientist but we now

believe that dark energy provides two levels of control, one via the rigid laws, the other by what we call 'nudges'. These ensure that the evolutionary process stays on track overall but give us considerable scope for doing our own thing.'

'There are so many questions! but the first in the queue in my over-working mind is this. Are you claiming that in some sense we are self-creating?'

Sallorna's face indicated that she was all too aware of the complexity of the issue which Terro-arwah had raised. The Gombranian responded with an enigmatic smile.

'I accept,' Sallorna said, 'that this is a difficult notion for linear thinkers. How can an effect be the cause that produces that effect? But we have found that the drive to think in a scientific, linear way is programmed into us. Without science humans could never have gained power. Those who had a strong drive to think in classical cause and effect terms were the ones who survived. But we also have to acknowledge the impossibility of infinity and eternity. No purely linear account of the universe is viable so we have to accept circularity. As I said before, it takes practice but it becomes easier with use.'

'I'm by no means convinced but I'll let that thread go for a while because there's the next query in the queue is about virtual time. You say that from a physical point of view it's in two segments but that to Alphomans, if I may call them that, it seems like one existence because there is no perception of the break.'

Sallorna nodded vigorously and said; 'Well put.'

'But we also exist, more or less fleetingly, for part of

Nature. In your natural lives you and your colleagues have formed the theory about Alphoma but, if I may turn things around, what might our Alphoma selves know about Nature?

'Oh, in Alphoma everything is known. It is possible to visit, examine, enjoy every aspect of Nature but it will be like a process or a picture or a structure; not something in which Alphomans can participate.'

'So, no secrets?'

'No, and none needed.'

'And no communication between Alphoma selves and Nature selves?'

'None.'

There was another long period of contemplation. Sallorna wondered if she were pushing the pace too quickly but her sense was that her listener had become eager.

'Tell me,' Terro-arwah said, 'all the people you left behind on Earth, are they long-time dead?'

'Not necessarily. We don't die unless we choose to. Perhaps one or two have stayed on but probably not. Even with guaranteed health and rich lives, people get weary and opt to take the quick route to Alphoma. And I'm fairly sure that if I were to take another three thousand years to get back there'd be nothing on Earth that would mean a great deal to me.'

Terro-arwah sighed and looked thoughtful.

'But I take it that you are not about to offer me new youth?'

Sallorna exuded apology.

'Terro-arwah, I'm sorry. We have thought deeply

about these things, even tried experiments on other planets but such gross interference always leads to disaster. We need to be subtle, we have to ensure that the process of evolution is not significantly distorted. Will power has to emerge; cooperation and understanding have to grow organically.'

Terro-arwah nodded. 'I knew as much of course', shee said. 'It was but natural wistfulness. But why should I care? If what you say is true I shall die and then be instantly in Alphoma.'

'The best way to look at things which also happens to be true,' Sallorna said.

The Gombranian made what appeared to be a conscious effort to lighten the discussion.

'You know, I have been thinking about all these profound things but a thought just popped into my head which might seem trivial.'

Sallorna invited herim to reveal the thoughts, glad also of a change of intensity.

'Well, might it be that the idea of a cosmic break up and reconstruction could account for the human love of puzzles. Presumably Gombranians are not alone in this?'

Sallorna was pleased with this contribution. Things, she thought, were going exceedingly well and she blessed the scientists who had made the last night's virtual experience possible.

'No, you are by no means alone.' she replied. 'There are examples throughout the Alliance. Most planets have jigsaw puzzles just as you do. There's also a widespread pastime for two which on Earth is called 'cat's cradle'. It involves string and starts with something simple, gets very complicated and then reverts to the original simplicity. It's found in very many cultures.'

'So the thought's not new then?'

'Remember what our respective ancient thinkers suggested; in a way there are no new thoughts.'

She could see that, fired though shee was, Terro-arwah was also getting tired. Shee was, after all, subject to ageing and had been alive for almost eighty Gombranian years.

'Let's stop for today,' Sallorna suggested. Her companion waved in agreement but said that shee wanted to give advance notice of the next question.

'It's this,' Terro-arwah said.

'I think you are claiming that everyone who existed, exists or will exist in Nature is also in Alphoma?'

Sallorna signalled her approval.

'How can this be? We die, we rot or are burned, we cease to exist. Surely we are gone forever?'

Sallorna brushed away a few strands of hair that had fallen across her eyes and she saw that Terro-arwah observed the gesture with interest, perhaps even with an awakening fondness.

'Excellent,' she said. 'Let's talk of all such things tomorrow,'

○ ○ ◯ ◯ ◯ ○ ○

Even though Sallorna arrived early the following morning Terro-arwah was waiting. Shee seemed to be in excellent spirits.

'I was thinking, during the night, of something that Gombranians can do which you Earthlings couldn't.'

Knowing that the mood was light, Sallorna said, 'Go on then, challenge me.'

Terro-arwah smiled and moved heris four upper limbs simultaneously to pluck almost perfectly spherical fruit from a nearby tree. Shee then began to juggle, starting sedately and building pace, throwing and catching with faultless accuracy. Sallorna laughed, feeling girlish in her delight. 'Astonishing!' she cried. 'I capitulate! Not even the best Earthly circus performer could match that!'

Slightly out of breath, Terro-arwah tossed the fruit into the foliage and sat down. 'Misspent youth,' shee gasped. 'I indulged myself with a few years as an entertainer, travelling, seeing as much of the world as I could. I haven't juggled for years but remnants of the skill are still with me.'

'Not remnants!' Sallorna protested, 'and nothing will persuade me to try to emulate that feat.'

There was a slightly awkward transition from the playful to the serious which Terro-arwah ended with a blunt question.

'So,' shee said, 'how do we live again?'

Sallorna began by talking about causation. 'Everything that happens,' she was soon saying, 'has traceable effects, even if the cause is an act of will.'

'True.'

'In fact, there's a fantastically complex chain of causes and effects which began at the big bang.'

'But surely the tracing task would be impossible. How could so much data be processed?'

Sallorna was ever trying to play down the gulf between Alliance knowledge and that of the Itrakians but at this point she felt she had no option but to explain about computers, about nano-technology and all the other science-based developments. Terro-arwah was indeed astonished.

'So in principle you, or of course I should say we, could map out the entire process of history?'

'The project had been started before I left Earth.'

'So we could know the details of what was in a person's brain at the time of death?'

'Yes.'

'And your wonderful technology allows you to reproduce brains?'

'Indeed. We have decided on ethical grounds not to do this until we are closer to the re-creation of Alphoma but yes, we could bring anyone back to life.'

'This is both inspirational and alarming.'

'It's reality.'

The teacher sensed that her pupil was beginning to feel emotional and, rather than see herim embarrassed, she suggested a short break. Terro-arwah was instantly against the idea. Sallorna moved her hands in a gesture of acceptance.

'But even so, you are talking about the re-creation of unimaginable numbers of people, not to mention all the other levels of consciousness of which you spoke; where will all these bodies be, where will they find sustenance?

'There will be no bodies, Terro-arwah,' Sallorna answered gently, 'bodies are of the physical universe whereas we will be returning to the mental. Already, even in its imperfect form, virtual reality is almost as immediate as the physical one.'

'It becomes clearer,' Terro-arwah said. 'The physical aspect will be relatively small, just something like the computers you were telling me about.'

'Yes, but it will be organic, a super-brain.'

A small flock of brilliantly coloured birds swooped and settled in a nearby tree. The noise of their chatter reminded Sallorna of Earth. She and the Gombranian remained silent for a while, an interlude which was ended by Terro-arwah.

'But why would you, or rather we if you insist, want to revive people?'

Sallorna paused for a few moments, framing her reply. She then said:

'Please recall what I said about everything being made of energy.'

'How could I forget?'

'Well, everything that happens in the universe does so via energy flow.'

'I've been thinking a great deal about energy and I'll accept that.'

'Good. Then the next step in the argument is that every time physical energy is expended the total stock of available energy in the universe is diminished, often ever so slightly, but it is the case that there is always less energy available for the future. Your mighty sun, which sustains all life on Gombran, is like a vast fire which one day will run out of fuel.'

Despite the warmth of the morning, Terro-arwah shivered.

'We had not thought of such things,' shee said. 'The conclusion must be that the universe will run down, getting ever cooler, until all life dies.'

'That would be the conclusion,' Sallorna said with a surge of brightness, 'if it were true that the universe is purely a physical phenomenon. But it isn't. It's also mental. And there is a source of energy associated with the activity of the mind.'

'Will power.'

Sallorna smiled at heris quickness of thought and said: 'Precisely.'

The Itrakian seemed pleased by the tacit praise.

'So we need consciousness to generate the power?'

Sallorna nodded.

'And Alphoma relies on this mental power?'

'Utterly.'

Terro-arwah lapsed into deep thought and, having learned heris pattern, Sallorna remained silent. The Gombranian ended the pause with a new idea.

'But you previously said that Alphoma contains all consciousness? Surely it could not encompass those beings we call 'evil', those who have gone often violently against the values of love and truth?'

Sallorna held her hands downwards, palms facing out, in a gesture of universal acceptance. She said:

'We need all consciousness because otherwise Alphoma would not be the complete universe but in any case we have long since moved away from the notion of evil. There are undeniably actions which are against the movement towards greater love but we do not judge any individual.'

'But do not some deserve to be punished?'

'If anyone feels guilty they punish themselves. If they feel no guilt they cannot be punished because they feel they have done no wrong.'

'But surely, people who have acted unlovingly will not be in a state to participate in Alphoma without going through a process of change.'

'We agree with that. Indeed, all of us will probably have to go through some transition process.'

'Just like some religions suggest.'

'Indeed. We believe that religions, though inaccurate in many respects, usually convey some truths. After all, they derive from introspection and they are also supported by very many thoughtful people over very long periods of time; their ideas are not to be taken unreservedly lightly.'

'But why a process? Why not, when recreating people, change them so that they are ready for Alphoma?'

'Because they would then not be the same people. One way of putting it is that they wouldn't recognise themselves. In any case, recall that we need to maximise will power. Change thus has to be voluntary. But we are very confident that there will be no problem with this, for once people have seen what Alphoma offers, that is, freedom to do and experience absolutely anything and everything, there will be no hesitation in wanting it to come about.'

Terro-arwah said that shee had many further questions but that shee could no longer deny that shee was getting tired. Sallorna gladly agreed to suspend the discussion until the following morning.

○ ○ ◯ ◯ ◯ ○ ○

Inevitably Terro-arwah had been pondering during the remainder of the previous day.

'Sallorna,' shee said, 'I have a very fundamental question to start this morning's proceedings.'

Sallorna said she was delighted and would do her best to answer.

'Well, it's the age-old conundrum as I'm sure you have guessed.'

'That is; where does the whole thing come from?' Sallorna suggested. Terro-arwah gestured heris agreement and congratulations.

'Nothing made it. This is all there is. This is the description of existence. As we have discussed, and I think more or less agreed, there cannot be a 'first cause' because, if we are thinking in causal terms, such a cause would itself have to have a cause.'

Terro-arwah shook heris head and said; 'Intellectually I accept this but it is so difficult to quell the insistent causal question.'

'I'm sure this is so,' Sallorna said, 'but please take my word that with logic as a tool it is possible to engineer a change of mental habit.'

'We'll see,' Terro-arwah said, 'but in the meantime, settle something for me.'

'Gladly.'

'It's something I have been thinking much about for the past few days. Suppose I accept that there can be no first cause there is still the question as to why the universal system has to have these two phases of Alphoma and Nature. Why is it not possible to have just Alphoma and to cut out the suffering?'

Sallorna smiled once more.

'It's similar to the question that is put to many religious leaders. Why does your wonderful god, who supposedly loves humans, create a world with so much misery?'

'Well?' Terro-arwah said with some force.

'Well! One thing to be borne in mind is that if there were no opposites there could be no meaning. For there to be love there has to be at least the idea of hate, for there to be peace there has to be conflict. This, we are sure, is one of the reasons why the universe has to have two phases.

'But it's much more than this. For there to be will-power, which is essential for existence, there have to be choices. And this implies that there will be destructive as well as creative choices.'

'Yet how can you know that the whole thing will work out. If there is free will, as you say, surely there can be overall destruction.'

'Not so, simply because if the outcome is destruction then there could be no existence.'

'But this implies that, despite what you said about dark energy and nudges, there is no freedom. The outcome is guaranteed!'

'Overall, yes; there is such a guarantee. But within the system, as I said, individuals have choice.'

'I still find this very difficult.'

Sallorna thought for a moment before saying:

'Imagine a tube which has been completely emptied

of all matter. At one end of the tube a cloud of dense gas is introduced. This cloud stays together but the individual particles from which it is made dash about in all directions. A very gentle force pushes the cloud forwards to the other end of the tube. It drifts towards a guaranteed destination but within the cloud there are particles which attempt to retreat, which interfere with the forward progress of others and which seem, generally, to be opposed to the other particles.

Terro-arwah thought for a while then said; 'There is much for me to ponder but alas I have a busy day ahead of me. I will think of all these things whenever I have time but when we next meet, tomorrow I trust, I want you to explain how it is that we, so far behind your Alliance in our thinking and technology, can be of the least assistance.'

○ ○ ◯ ◯ ◯ ○ ○

The next day, Terro-arwah promptly reminded heris visitor of the agenda for the morning. Sallorna said that she had by no means forgotten. She began:

'I have doubtless given you the strong impression that the Alliance is almighty but our power is still limited. There will have been massive advances since I left Earth but I have no doubt that even with these we have to be careful how we proceed. The truth is that for all our progress, all of the Alliance planets have come close to disaster.'

'What kind of disaster?'

'Well, there's an object lesson in a planet very close

to Earth, one we call Venus, which was once a seeming paradise where evolution made relatively rapid progress. Humans emerged much earlier than they did on Earth but alas they were unaware of the consequences of some of their actions. They produced too many damaging materials from their manufacturing processes, the planet began to heat up and very swiftly it was out of control, paradise turned into an inferno.'

'It seems impossible,' Terro-arwah said with a shudder, 'we are so puny compared to nature.'

'That's how it seemed to them,' Sallorna said, 'until it was too late. We almost suffered the same fate on Earth. The good news is that we discovered, just in time. a way of reversing the heating process. My own planet was saved and when I left it was being predicted that, thanks to a massive restoration project, within a few hundred years life on Venus would once more be possible.'

'So perhaps it is flourishing now, given all the time you spent on your journey?'

'I trust so,' Sallorna replied, 'but whether or not planets such as Venus can be restored, the fact is that millions of humans perished there under terrible circumstances. There are many other examples of disaster coming from incomplete knowledge. The Alliance decided, many, many years ago that a balance had to be struck between respecting the freedom of others and the prevention of unnecessary suffering.'

'Perhaps you mean that they, or I should say you, want to speed up the process of re-creating Alphoma?'

'Some, perhaps, but not most of us. Time becomes irrelevant when one can choose to live or die knowing that Alphoma is instantly attainable.'

'So,' Terro-arwah said after a long period of thought, 'the Alliance sent out people like you to contact people like me to help us to avoid disaster.'

'Yes, and to set up regional centres from which your successors can reach out so as to save others from needless suffering. As I left Earth we had not completely solved the problems of rapid travel and quick long-distance communication. Judging by the lack of other Alliance presence here on Gombran there must still be problems. Maybe they will never be solved, in which case the kind of task which I am performing will be the only way of communication until the universe begins to contract.'

'You think there might be human life on nearby planets?' Terro-arwah asked.

'It is very likely, according to our predictions, though Gombran seemed the most promising. But certainly there are planets which, in maybe a few hundred years time, your successors could visit with an expectation of finding self-conscious beings.'

'And how many ambassadors, if I may call you that, have been despatched by your alliance?

'Oh, thousands, literally thousands.'

'More candles in the darkness?'

'Perhaps.'

'But why have you come alone? Surely it would have been all the better to have had some companions?'

'There might have been advantages but we needed to conserve. Even with the most advanced technology available at the time I left, there were limitations. In any case, I am happy to be the sole ambassador to your lovely planet. And if I get lonely I have a wonderful simulator on my spacecraft which can take me, with almost total reality, back to my beloved Earth.'

'Would that I could see this,' Terro-arwah said.

Sallorna shrugged. 'Alas my shuttle is designed for one but in any case the rules of my mission would not permit this.'

'I guessed as much. But enough of aspirations, I need to know how things might be done. What are you proposing? I am close to the end of my life and you have already made it clear that you are not proposing to grant me a reprieve from natural death.'

Sallorna shook her head in a gesture of regret. 'No. As I said, we have tried such tactics on other planets and direct action such as that has always created problems.'

'Then what?'

'We have prepared a well-tested strategy. The first thing will be for you to talk to others whom you trust. Of course there will be scepticism at first but when the time is right I will speak to them and prove that what you are saying is true.

'Then, when they are reconciled and agreed, I will arrange for information to be transferred to your brain and to theirs. You will have the basis, both in technical terms and in those of good governance, to move rapidly forward. Once that process has started I will leave you, because freedom is of the utmost value.'

'You will leave to die?'

Sallorna smiled. 'Well, she said, 'I might linger for a while to see how you fare, then arrange another period of coma so that I can intervene again in a few hundred or thousand years time if need be but then, yes, once I am confident that things are moving in the right direction I will choose the re-birth into Alphoma where life will be untroubled and I can embrace all my loved ones.'

'And if I refuse to cooperate?'

'Then I will seek someone else in another part of Gombran and continue searching until the seed is sown.'

'Surely you could coerce me, or even programme my brain.'

'Indeed we could, but that would be of no use. Remember will-power is the essential ingredient.'

Terro-arwah closed all four of heris eyes and was silent for a long time. Shee then said; 'This is a dreadful responsibility which you put upon me.'

Sallorna agreed. 'Yet this is the way which we have found has the best chance of success. But, as I said, if you feel disinclined there will almost certainly be others who will take up the burden. I can even, if you so wish, erase all memory of our conversations from your mind. If someone else takes up the challenge and begins to speak of me you will be as sceptical as everyone else.'

The Gombranian thought for a long time. Sallorna was delighted that when shee spoke it was as though the offer of the memory-wipe had not been heard.

'Sallorna, what you have told me is monumental, so testing to the imagination but there is one major difficulty.'

Shee paused. Sallorna waited, as she had learned to do. Terro-arwah broke the silence.

'The big bang, the expansion and contraction,

the emergence of consciousness, the gradual assumption of control; all of these things and others I can grasp but I struggle with this notion of mental energy. What does that mean? How can Alphoma exist?'

Sallorna nodded. 'It is difficult. To explain it I will need to tell you about more of our science.'

Terro-arwah smiled. 'Could you not just save me the labour and feed the information directly into my brain?' shee asked.

'Indeed, I could,' Sallorna replied with a jocular nod, 'but our strict policy is not to do any direct feeding until all the arguments have been presented and the chosen person has agreed to the entire scheme.'

'I suppose that's honourable.' Terro-arwah said with a sigh. 'So I'm going to have to work.' Heris expression indicated humorous resignation.

'I'll make it as easy as I can,' said Sallorna with a delighted laugh.

She then treated her distinguished pupil to an account of electro-magnetism and radiation. Fortunately the Itrakians were the Gombranian inventors of the compass so Terro-arwah was familiar with the principles of magnetism. There was also a level of understanding of natural electrical phenomena so the journey to understanding was not too arduous. Before too long Sallorna was able to say;

'As energy becomes more organised, more physically complex, it generates a field of radiation around it. With material objects these fields are small although, for example, trees have forces around them which some humans can sense. But it is only when we move higher up the evolutionary path that the fields become really significant.'

'And ultimately so in humans?' suggested Terro-arwah, who was keenly listening.

'Yes, precisely. The human brain is an electrical device with a power which we can measure. It produces a field which in some planetary civilisations is visible. Indeed, some Earthlings claim to be able to perceive auras but mostly we cannot. They are, however, detectable with instruments.'

Terro-arwah was nodding affirmatively. 'There are Itrakians who say that we all have auras. Some allege that they can derive information from them.'

'Probably with good reason,' Sallorna responded. 'We have evidence that the fields contain data and that when two of them come together, as when humans touch head to head, there is sometimes significant, largely unconscious, communication. There is also the phenomenon when people get together in large numbers at sports events or performances of drama or music whereby there is a kind of multiplier effect. Instead of being separate, as they usually are, the brain fields begin to merge and emotions become accordingly heightened. Alas the phenomenon has been used by demagogues and some religious leaders to very harmful effect.'

Terro-arwah nodded. 'We know to our cost too!' shee said and paused for a few moments of reflection before saying;

'And these fields, I suppose you are about to tell me, are associated with conscious activity.'

'Indeed. We know that there is energy movement

within them and that these movements are particularly associated with efforts of will.'

'Have you established a science of their operation?'

Sallorna smiled. 'That's the interesting aspect. Energy movements within the fields are not scientifically predictable. The only information we have about them is what people report of their conscious activity. We can detect brain changes which come about as a result of such activity but they are ephemeral and unquantifiable we cannot predict them. This is largely why we think of consciousness as inhering in the brain fields.'

Terro-arwah lapsed into one of heris long silences. At last shee said; 'It's hard to digest but it's also thrilling. I can't help thinking of juggling. The brain keeps the balls of consciousness in the air. When the brain stops, so does consciousness.'

Sallorna laughed outright. 'What a lovely analogy!' she declared, 'it'll stay in my mind.'

'Glad to have been of influence,' Terro-arwah said with a wry smile, 'but you are suggesting that the balls develop a life of their own, which indeed sometimes they seem to do.'

'Well,' said Sallorna, still smiling, 'it doesn't do to take analogies too far but I like the idea of our conscious selves as being your looping fruit.'

'Good,' said Terro-arwah, heris face portraying a return to seriousness, 'but pray continue. I'm ready to take the next steps.'

Sallorna composed herself before saying:

'So the activity in the brain creates a radiation field, a kind of globe. This alters the energy in the immediate vicinity.'

'Are the environmental changes permanent?'

'Yes they are, though usually they are tiny and extremely difficult to detect. But they are also cumulative, energy is being changed all the time as a result of conscious activity.'

'But these brain fields must have mass, they are to some extent physical phenomena?'

'Yes, they do have very tiny mass'

'So that when someone dies, that mass dissipates.'

'Indeed, but bear in mind that most people shut down thought processes gradually as death approaches because that generally is the effect of illness but, yes, anyone coming to a sudden end has a swift loss of field.'

'This perhaps is where the idea of the departure of a soul comes from.'

'Very likely, but it is not an entity which floats off and exists elsewhere, it is an activity which ceases.'

'So much is understood but I think you have also suggested, earlier in our discourse, that whilst they exist, these fields have a power of their own. They depend upon brains for existence but some of their driving force is self generated.'

Sallorna was delighted with this intervention and her expression conveyed pleasure. Terro-arwah looked at her and smiled. It seemed that both were aware of a surge of well-being. 'Maybe our force fields merged a little,' Terro-arwah said softly. Sallorna responded. 'I'm sure they just did.'

She felt some confusion and asked the Gombranian to repeat the comment about self-generation. She then answered;

'Yes, the exercise of will power, the processes of conscious thought, are power generators; they reverse the physical run-down of energy.'

'Can this be proven?'

'In the laboratory yes. There have been volunteers who have agreed to have all their data transferred to an inert, artificial brain. When this is subsequently activated we can measure the energy flows.

'There was a much bigger experiment in the planning stage as I left on my journey,' Sallorna continued. 'Alliance scientist were working on what we call a pre-Alphoma trial. The idea is to feed the personal data of many people into a highly efficient brain which will be contained in a sphere filled with an inert gas. It is predicted that after the initial charge to start the system the sustaining energy input from outside will drop dramatically. The sphere will be filled with mental activity which will feed into the brain.'

'Real people?' Terro-arwah asked in astonishment.

Yes, volunteers who are very willing to give the virtual life a try.'

'And will they continue in the virtual world?'

'No, the experiment is time-limited. Some of the volunteers will be restored to their natural lives, others will probably choose to die.'

'But the need for external energy input will not disappear entirely?' Terro-arwah asked, heris scientific curiosity fully aroused.

'No, but neither would we expect it to; that will happen only when all the energy of the universe is brought together in Alphoma. Our calculations show that there is a critical point and this is why we need all of the available consciousness.'

Terro-arwah nodded as though an expectation had been confirmed.

'I'm sorry that you had to leave before the experiment could be conducted,' Terro-arwah said, 'I would give much to know the outcome.'

'Me too', Sallorna said, 'but Gombran was of higher priority.'

'For which I am truly grateful,' Terro-arwah replied. Shee indicated that there was a need for the customary thinking time and was silent for longer than usual.

'And yet,' shee said as though there had been no pause. 'I still find it almost impossible to imagine how the vastness of the universe, so much greater than we had imagined if what you tell me is correct, can be brought together in your Omega process.'

Sallorna nodded in acknowledgement of the weightiness of the question.

'We, all of us in the universe, will cooperate to create local centres modelled on the final state. Imagine, if you will, huge spheres of sparkling, glowing, almost weightless substance with a tiny core, the source of the gentle gravity which keeps the units together.

'The clouds will merge, the organic computers with them. According to the designed pattern, the cores will congregate, ready for the final integration. At the moment of fusion, the mighty moment, a peaceful, glorious, joyous happening which will be the very antithesis of the cosmic explosion, the units will lock together and Alphoma will be formed. There will be a celestial glowing, the last physical display, and then there will be darkness.'

'But light within?'

'Light upon light, life upon life. Timeless bliss for all.'

'To be followed by the explosion?'

'No,' Sallorna said. 'It is necessary to change one's thinking. The account of the universe has to be self-contained. We still have strong instincts to see things linearly but the framework is once and for all, static and magnificent.'

Terro-arwah pondered further. Sallorna waited, feeling that the fate of her mission was in the balance. Of course there would be other possibilities but she knew that there were no other thinkers of the calibre of her chosen one.

'Sallorna,' shee said eventually, 'I have much to consider. Please indulge me with a night and a day of cogitation. For a change, visit me tomorrow evening when the air is cooler and the flowers will be treating us to their exotic scents. You will bring me more Earthly music and then will I tell you of my decision.'

The Earthling smiled serenely and said; 'So be it.'

There was a guideline for outreach agents that initially the use of technology should be kept to a minimum but already Sallorna had given herself permission to use a minute player which contained all the music known to the Alliance. Terro-arwah had specified something from her native planet. The obvious challenge was what she should choose.

She waved farewell and softly called kalyeka.

Something in her host's demeanour spoke to her.

'Schubert' she said to herself decisively as she turned to walk away.

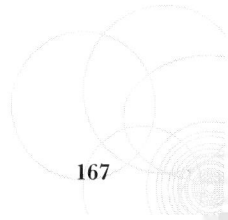

○ ○ ◯ ◯ ◯ ○ ○

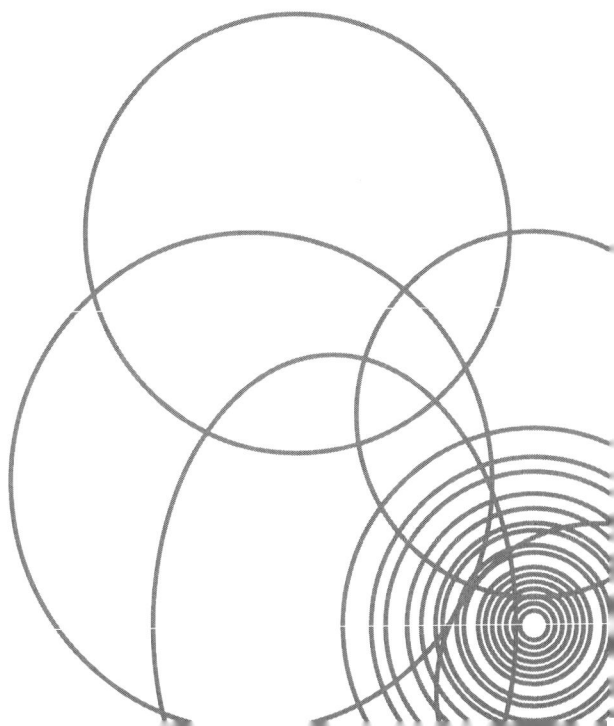